Remembering Belsen

Remembering Belsen:
Eyewitnesses Record the Liberation
is published in association with the
Holocaust Educational Trust.

BCM Box 7892, London WC1N 3XX

Telephone: 020 7222 6822; Fax: 020 7233 0161

Email: info@het.org.uk

Website: www.het.org.uk

Remembering Belsen

Eyewitnesses Record the Liberation

Editors

Ben Flanagan
Donald Bloxham

Foreword by

Lord Campbell of Croy

VALLENTINE MITCHELL
LONDON • PORTLAND, OR

First published in 2005 in Great Britain by
VALLENTINE MITCHELL
Suite 314, Premier House, 112–114 Station Road,
Edgware, Middlesex HA8 7BJ
and in the United States of America by
VALLENTINE MITCHELL
c/o ISBS, 920 NE 58th Avenue, Suite 300,
Portland, OR 97213 3786
Portland, Oregon, 97213-3644

Website http://www.vmbooks.com

British Library Cataloging in Publication Data:

A catalogue record for this book has been applied for

ISBN 0 85303 604 7 (cloth)
ISBN 0 85303 605 5 (paper)

Library of Congress Cataloging-in-Publication Data:

A catalog record for this book has been applied for

Typeset by FiSH Books, London
Printed in Great Britain by MPG Books Ltd, Bodmin, Cornwall

Contents

List of Plates

21 An expert shoe-maker working in the corner of his room in Bergen-Belsen Displaced Persons' Camp.
22 The first train for Palestine draws out from the very siding at Belsen to which many people were brought by the Nazis.

All photographs courtesy of the Institute of Contemporary History and Wiener Library, London.

Foreword

Bergen-Belsen was the only major Nazi concentration camp to be liberated on the British front, some three weeks before the end of the war in Europe in 1945. This book contains accounts which should ensure that the horrors of the camp are on the record for posterity and cannot be denied or excused.

I welcome its publication because on 15 April 1945 I was a major in the 15th Scottish Infantry Division advancing across north Germany with the 11th Armoured Division. As described in this volume by Brigadier Glyn-Hughes, the senior military medical officer in our advancing columns, staff officers had received a warning from the Germans that there was a source of dangerous disease ahead. The enormity of the situation became apparent only when the British arrived in Belsen.

My division was engaged in fighting and finishing the war and we moved on to continue the advance to the Elbe and the Baltic. (I was wounded in our last major battle, the assault crossing of the River Elbe, resulting in a very long time in hospital.) Word had quickly passed round our soldiers about what had been found at Belsen, however, and any doubts that existed about why we were at war were quickly ended.

Later it was recognised that Brigadier Glyn-Hughes had carried out a remarkably efficient operation in Belsen given the short notice. As many lives as possible were saved among the surviving inmates and immediate measures were applied to contain disease and relieve starvation. It was sad that the brigadier died soon after the war, but I am sure all who knew him at that time remember him with admiration.

Although Soviet forces discovered Majdanek, Auschwitz and other camps on their front in 1944–45, the significance of these sites did not register in the West until much later. It was the atrocities perpetrated at Belsen and Buchenwald, therefore, that became headline news in the Western press in April 1945. The eyewitness reports and testimonies are as profoundly shocking today as they were then; they are gathered in this volume so that they will not be forgotten.

The Rt. Hon. Lord Campbell of Croy, PC, MC

Richard Dimbleby's Despatch
of 17 April 1945*

I have just returned from the Belsen concentration camp, where for two hours I drove slowly about the place in a jeep, with the Chief Doctor of the Second Army [. . .] I find it hard to describe adequately the horrible things I have seen and heard today. But here, unadorned, are the facts.

There are 40,000 men, women and children in the camp, German and half-a-dozen other nationalities, thousands of them Jews. Of this [. . .] 4,250 are acutely ill or dying of virulent disease. Typhus, typhoid, diphtheria, dysentery, pneumonia and childbirth fever are rife. 25,600, three-quarters of them women, are either ill from lack of food or are actually dying of starvation. In the last few months alone 30,000 prisoners have been killed off or allowed to die [. . .] I wish with all my heart that everyone fighting in this war, and above all those whose duty it is to direct the war from Britain and America, could have come with me through the barbed wire fence that leads to the inner compound of the camp... beyond the barrier was a swirling cloud of dust, the dust of thousands of slowly-moving people, laden in itself with the deadly typhus germ. And with the dust was a smell, sickly and thick, the smell of death and decay, of corruption and filth.

I passed through the barrier and found myself in the world of nightmare. Dead bodies, some of them in decay, lay strewn about the road and along the rutted track. On each side of the road were brown wooden huts. There were faces at the windows, the bony emaciated faces of starving women, too weak to come outside, propping themselves against the glass to see the daylight before they died. And they were dying every hour and every minute. I saw a man, wandering dazedly along the road, stagger and fall. Someone else looked down at him, took him by the heels and dragged him to the side of the road to join the other bodies lying unburied there. No-one else took the slightest notice. They didn't even trouble to turn their heads. Behind the huts two youths and two girls, who'd found a morsel of food, were sitting together on the grass in picnic fashion, sharing it. They were not six feet from a pile of decomposing bodies. [...]

I have seen many terrible sights in the last five years, but nothing, nothing approaching the dreadful interior of this hut in Belsen. The dead and the dying lay close together. I picked my way over corpse after corpse in the gloom until I heard one voice that rose above the gentle undulating moaning. I found a girl. She was a living skeleton. Impossible to gauge her age because she had practically no hair left on her head and her face was only a yellow parchment sheet with two holes in it for eyes. She was stretching out her stick of an arm and gasping something. It was 'English, English. Medicine, medicine,' and she was trying to cry, but had not enough strength. And beyond her, down the passage and in the hut, there were the convulsive movements of dying people too weak to raise themselves from the floor. They were crawling with lice and smeared with filth. They'd had no food for days, for the Germans sent it down into the camp *en bloc* and only those strong enough to come out of the huts could get it. The rest of them lay in the shadows growing weaker and weaker. There was no one to take the bodies away when they died and I had to look hard to see who was alive and who was dead. [...]

In the shade of some trees lay a great collection of bodies [...] There were perhaps 150, flung down on each other, all naked, all so thin their yellow skin glistened like stretched rubber on their bones. Some of the poor starved creatures [...] looked so utterly unreal and inhuman that I could've imagined that they'd never lived at all. They were like polished skeletons. [...]

Babies were born at Belsen, some of them shrunken, wizened little things that could not live, because their mothers could not feed them. One woman, distraught to the point of madness, flung herself at a British soldier [...] She begged him to give her some milk for the tiny baby she held in her arms. She laid the mite on the ground, threw herself at the sentry's feet and kissed his boots. When, in his distress, he asked her to get up she put the baby in his arms and ran off crying that she would find milk for it as there was no milk in her breast. And when the soldier opened the bundle of rags to look at the child he found it had been dead for days.

I have never seen British soldiers so moved to cold fury as the men who opened the Belsen camp this week and those of the police and RAMC who are now on duty trying to save the prisoners who are not too far gone in starvation. The SS guards who shot several of the prisoners after we had arrived in the camp when they thought no one was looking are now gathering up all the bodies and carting them away for burial.

As we went deeper into the camp [...] I realised that what is so ghastly is not so much the individual acts of barbarism [...] but the gradual breakdown of civilisation that happens when human beings are herded like animals behind barbed wire. Here in Belsen we were seeing people, many of them lawyers, doctors, chemists, musicians, authors, who'd long since ceased to care about the conventions or the customs of normal life. There had been no privacy of any kind. Women stood naked at the side of the track, washing in cupfuls of water taken from British Army water trucks. Others squatted while they searched themselves for lice and examined each other's hair. Sufferers from dysentery leaned against the huts straining helplessly, and all around and about them was this awful drifting tide of exhausted people, neither caring nor watching. Just a few held out their withered hands to us as we passed by [...] Back in the hut by the main gate of the camp I questioned the sergeant who'd been in charge of one of the SS squads. He was a fair-haired gangling creature with tiny crooked ears rather like Goebbels and big hands [...] I asked him how many people he had killed. He looked vacant for a moment then replied 'Oh, I don't remember...'

Every fact I've so far given you has been verified but there is one more awful than all the others that I've kept to the end. Far away in the corner of the Belsen camp there is a pit, the size of a tennis court, it's 15 foot deep and at the end it's piled to the very top with naked bodies that have been tumbled in one on top of the other. Like this must have been the plague pits in England 300 years ago, only nowadays we can help by digging them quicker with bulldozers and already there's a bulldozer at work in Belsen. Our army doctors examining some of these bodies found in their sides a long slit, apparently made by someone with surgical knowledge. They made enquiries and they established beyond doubt that in the frenzy of their starvation [some of] the people of Belsen had taken the wasted bodies of their fellow prisoners and had removed from them the only remaining flesh, the liver and the kidneys, to eat.

May I add to this story only the assurance that everything that an army can do to save these men, women and children is being done, and that those officers and men who've seen these things have gone back to the Second Army moved to an anger such as I have never seen in them before.

*From a typescript held at the BBC Written Archives Centre (WRU C7726). After a delay – caused by the disbelief of Dimbleby's colleagues in London – a heavily edited version was broadcast on 19 April 1945. Though perhaps the most 'famous' of all Belsen testimonies, popular confusion surrounds what was actually said in that broadcast. Crucially, it omitted Dimbleby's reference to the 'thousands of [...] Jews' who were liberated.

Acknowledgements

The publication of this volume was made possible by the generous support of Sir Arthur Gilbert, who died in 2001.

The project was initiated by Lord Janner of Braunstone, QC, Chairman of the Holocaust Educational Trust, London.

Jo Reilly, then of Southampton University, was vital in the emergence of the book. Along with the editors, she was intimately involved with the selection and editing of the testimonies, and in the writing of various introductory passages to the chapters. She also co-authored Chapter 8. Tony Kushner of Southampton University gave additional useful advice.

The editors owe much to the friendly and helpful staff at the Institute of Contemporary History and Wiener Library, London, the British Library, and the National Archives in Kew (formerly the Public Records Office). Particular thanks is due to the Trustees of the Imperial War Museum for allowing access to collections held at the Departments of Documents and Sound Archive. Use of the Wellcome Library for the History and Understanding of Medicine, the library of the Religious Society of Friends in Britain and the British Red Cross Museum and Archives was invaluable in gathering the testimony used in this volume.

The following publishers and publications kindly gave their permission to reproduce extracts in this volume: Giles de la Mare, I.B.Tauris, Duckworth, Methuen & Co. Ltd, Allen & Unwin, Halban and the *Jewish Chronicle*.

Editors' Note

All texts – memoirs, reports, letters – are presented here as in the original source and have been edited only lightly for sense. Many extracts, however, have had to be cut for reasons of space and to avoid repetition of factual information relating to the Belsen camp. An ellipsis in square brackets [...] marks such an editorial intervention.

UNTRACEABLE CONTRIBUTORS

From the papers of Captain J. Gant held at the Department of Documents at the Imperial War Museum (99/82/1). Efforts to contact the copyright holders of this document were unsuccessful. The editors of this volume would be most interested to hear from the writer's estate.

From the papers of Rev. Fr. Edmund Swift held at the Department of Documents at the Imperial War Museum (90/4/1). Father Swift died in 1992; his surviving family, the copyright holders of these documents, could not be traced. The editors of this volume would be most interested to hear from the writer's estate.

From the papers of Eryl Hall Williams held at the Department of Documents at the Imperial War Museum (93/27/2). With thanks to the Yearly Meeting of the Religious Society of Friends in Britain, which holds the copyright for documents written by Friends Relief Service workers.

From a photocopy of a letter by Enid Fernandes held by the British Red Cross Museum and Archives (AccX/104). No contact details for Fernandes or members of her family are held by the British Red Cross Museum and Archives; the editors of this volume would be most interested to hear from the writer's estate

From Robert Collis and Han Hogerzeil, *Straight On* (London: Methuen & Co. Ltd, 1947). Despite contacting Methuen Publishing Ltd, London, the copyright holder for these extracts could not be traced. The editors of this volume would be most interested to hear from the writer's estate.

From Anny Pfirter, Memories of a Red Cross Mission, held at the Wellcome Library (RAMC Box 270: RAMC 1218 / 2 / 18). No contact details for Pfirter or members of her family could be traced. The editors of this volume would be most interested to hear from the writer's estate.

Abbreviations

BLA	British Liberation Army
CCS	Casualty Clearing Station
DDMS	Deputy Director of Medical Services
DDT	dichlor-diphenyl-trichloroethane; powerful insecticide
DP	Displaced Person
MO	Medical Officer
OC	Officer Commanding
RA	Royal Artillery
RAMC	Royal Army Medical Corps
RSM	Regimental Sergeant Major
WVHA	SS Business Administration Main Office (Wirtschafts- und Verwaltungshauptamt)

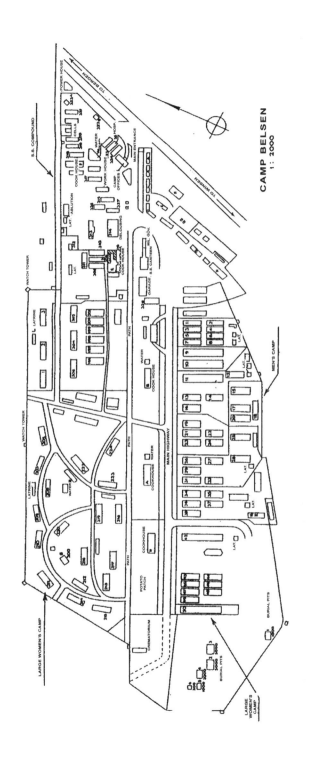

Map of Belsen drawn by Derrick Sington, one of the early liberators of the camp (from *Belsen Uncovered*, London: Duckworth, 1946)

Introduction

4 December 1944 At 10.00am the order came that at half past twelve 164 men from the diamond industry [brought to Belsen from Amsterdam] had to go on a transport *without* their wives and children. [...]

The parting was of the kind that is called heartrending. Many women and children cried, yet the majority controlled themselves very well. No one knows the destination of the transport.

[...]

[... T]his morning the news came that the wives and children of the men from the diamond industry were leaving. They have no provisions with them.

Will they be staying in the women's camp? And what will happen to the children? This is persecution! The refinement is unsurpassed.

Einmalig! [unique!]

[...]

In the evening We have just heard that the children have remained behind. Separated from their mothers.

The children are huddled together in the garage outside the main gate of the camp. They gave them white bread. How kind! A few older children are looking after them. Just now they came to fetch camp blankets for the children. Poor H. with your sweet little face, six years old! The children are unaware of anything. We know what will happen. I am not writing it down. After the war perhaps.

13 January 1945 Yesterday marked our first year here [in the 'Star camp' in Belsen]. It has been a terrible year, far from home, from the children, without news from them, a year of disappointment. The transport to Palestine [in which he was not included], the peace that did not come, a year of hunger, cold, hounding, persecution and humiliation.

7 March 1945　Recently I have come to learn the meaning of despair. I am ill again and have given up all hope of getting out of here. [...]

Hunger is increasing, and in the long run, the psychological burden in particular becomes unbearable. If only there were a means to end it all. I am afraid of the pain, of the death-struggle.

Every day the dying continues. I have fever.

22 March 1945 [...]　Last night a transport of two thousand people arrived from Buchenwald concentration camp. The shouting, abusing, crying, taunting, groaning, cracking of the whips and thuds of the beatings could be heard throughout the night.

This morning [...] we saw hundreds of corpses being dragged onto a heap and stripped of their clothing. They also removed the gold teeth from their mouths. Never has it been as bad as this. All day, the heap of emaciated, naked bodies was left lying in the sun.

Abel J. Herzberg, *diary written in Belsen*[1]

I am aged 23 and am a Jewess of Czecho-Slovakian nationality. I left the Sudetenland in September 1938 and went to Czecho-Slovakia. I was arrested by the Germans in Prague and on 23rd October 1941 was sent to the Ghetto in Poland. My mother and baby sister were gassed at the Ghetto and I, with the rest of the family, was transferred to Auschwitz. In August 1944, my father having been gassed at Auschwitz, I and my sister were transferred to Belsen Concentration Camp.

[...]

I was one of the first batch of a thousand girls to arrive at Belsen. [...] I was employed as a clerk and it was my duty to record the number of deaths of women in the camp each day. In the first few weeks the figures were low. As more internees arrived the deaths increased. In January, 15 to 20 died daily. From then on deaths increased until the last day of March, on which day the number of deaths reported was 349. This figure was not accurate since all deaths were not reported and bodies uncounted were lying in the open. In April the daily deaths increased but I can give no figures as I then went ill with typhus. I estimate that 900 of my party have died from malnutrition, disease and ill-treatment.

Katherine Neiger, *deposition sworn on 6 May 1945*[2]

April 1945 was exceptionally hot. I remember this well. It is sometimes difficult and sometimes easy, too easy, to remember things one would rather forget or suppress. But I can feel the oppressive heat now and smell the unbearably sweet smell of naked decomposing bodies, especially when I shut my eyes. Now half a century has gone by, and a new generation has grown up, a generation which is probably as bored of hearing about concentration camps as we were with the stories of the front line in the Great War that my father used to tell us. But I was going to talk about 15th April 1945, the day of the liberation.

Many of the events of the day are rather hazy but I remember certain details. In the morning I left my sister in the care of a comrade and went in search of water. Anita lay on a bunk, very sick, and was murmuring incomprehensible words. She had a high temperature. It could not be typhus because we had already had that in Auschwitz. But she was not in a good state. We had not had any bread for several days. The soup that was occasionally distributed in minute quantities was mainly water, and quite undrinkable. I had managed to 'organize' a rusty bucket and went to the camp entrance. There was an apparently harmless SS man standing guard, and he did not attempt to stop me. I was making for the one and only water tap that was still functioning. It was near the administration barracks and that was deserted.

The Germans had evaporated. No one at all stopped me. I filled my bucket and returned through the gate. There I was met by a horde of prisoners, half dead with thirst, trying to get hold of some of the water...The bucket was snatched from my hands, the precious liquid spilled into the dust and disappeared. It was a hopeless undertaking. I returned to my barracks empty-handed. I helped my sister off her bunk and led her out into the open air. We sat on the ground, leaning against the hut. In front of us...next to us...corpses.

[...]

A few days earlier the SS had tried to get a commando to move the bodies to a big ditch. We had been given some string to tie the arms of the dead together and then drag them along the main thoroughfare in the camp. But we did not have the strength. The 'operation' was discontinued and the bodies remained where they were.

Then it must have been mid-day. For days we had heard the rumbling noises of heavy artillery, but we hadn't known who was firing. We had had no idea what was happening to us. The noise came closer...and then...a voice through a loud-hailer...first in English and then in German. At the beginning we were too confused and excited to take anything in. But the announcements kept being repeated, again and again. At last we understood: BRITISH TROOPS ARE STANDING BY THE CAMP GATES...PLEASE KEEP CALM...YOU ARE LIBERATED...We were also told – and this was not news to us – that there was typhus in the camp, and that we should wait for the troops to come. We should be patient...medical help was on its way. It took a while for the significance of these announcements to sink in.

When the first tank finally rolled into the camp, we looked at our liberators in silence. We were deeply suspicious. We simply could not believe that we had not been blown up before the Allies could get to us.

Renate Lasker-Wallfisch, *survivor of Auschwitz and Belsen*[3]

*

These brief extracts from the testimonies of three individual survivors give some insight into the ghastly nature of the Bergen-Belsen camp during the final two years of the war and a clue to the complex role the camp played in the Nazi system. They are a fitting introduction to this collection, which, though not primarily concerned with documenting the war years, seeks to bring together a collection of little-known eyewitness testimonies that paint a vivid picture of the post-liberation period in Belsen. From numerous reports, testimonies, letters and memoirs written by survivors, soldiers and relief workers who experienced the liberated Belsen camp in 1945 or later, we gain a unique perspective on the rehabilitation operation and the development of Belsen into a Displaced Persons' Camp. Many of the testimonies gathered in this collection are taken from archives, and are previously unpublished or from books that are long out of print.

Bergen-Belsen was one of the first Nazi concentration camps to be liberated by the Western Allies and the only intact major camp to be liberated by the British army. In April and May 1945, the British people were exposed to a flood of information on the camps; Belsen, in particular, entered British consciousness for the first time through the unprecedented and disturbing images of the newly liberated camp. At no time in the previous four years had the press given to the extermination centres in Poland anything approaching the coverage and comment they now gave to the camps exposed in Germany. Belsen, along with Buchenwald, the latter particularly for the USA, dominated conversation and the newspaper letter pages. Wireless broadcasts, newspaper reports and newsreels triggered a wave of shock and horror across the whole country. Many have never forgotten the feelings evoked in them on seeing the newsreel footage of Belsen for the first time.

Yet despite this attention it is true to say that few people in 1945, including some of the soldiers on the ground, gained any real understanding of what had been the function of the camp or the nature of its development and the experience of the prisoners prior to the liberation. The British public fitted the camp within a pre-war narrative of Nazi punishment camps constructed on German soil to crush political opposition or deal with the criminal element within German society. Relatively few in Britain, despite graphic press reports and the protest of the House of Commons in 1942, had grasped the true nature of the Nazis' eastern Europe-centred wartime policy of genocide against the Jews, and even those who had done so would have had little reason to suspect that prisoners liberated in Belsen, hundreds of miles away, were witnesses to this policy. Indeed, in press and military reports on Belsen in April 1945 there are few mentions of Jewish people at all, and there is certainly no indication that almost half of the prisoners liberated alive were of Jewish origin.

The truth was that in 1944 the Nazis had turned the Belsen camp from a small-scale holding centre for prisoners – many, like Herzberg, from the Netherlands – whom they wanted to exchange for prominent Germans abroad, into a dumping ground for sick and emaciated camp prisoners and forced labourers from Poland and elsewhere in Germany. Katherine Neiger, originally from Czechoslovakia, and Anita Lasker-Wallfisch, born in Breslau, fell into this latter category. Having been deported to Auschwitz and survived the inhuman conditions there, they were forced back to the west and left to die in Belsen of starvation and disease. Those readers interested in a more detailed description of the history of Belsen and the reasons for this transformation from 'exchange' camp to 'horror' camp in just 12 months will find it in Chapter 8, 'The Belsen Camp in Historical Context'.

The focus of the collection, however, is on the liberation period. Chapters 1 to 3 chart the relief efforts of the various agencies working in Belsen and the impact of their work on the prisoners, while the evolution of the site from a place of death and destruction to a thriving Jewish Displaced Persons' Camp, a community of over 10,000 people forging a future for themselves, is the focus of Chapters 4 and 5. Chapter 6 examines the proceedings of the Belsen trial in western Europe, the first Holocaust-related war crimes trial, which began in September 1945, and Chapter 7 seeks to explore an as yet little-studied theme: the relationship between the Belsen camp and the local German community and the place of the site in post-war memorial culture and politics. Each chapter comprises a short contextual introduction followed by a range of eyewitness views.

NOTES

1. Abel J. Herzberg, *Between Two Streams: A Diary from Bergen-Belsen*, trans. Jack Santcross (London: I.B.Tauris, 1997), p. 172–4, 190, 201, 204.
2. Public Records Office, WO 235/24.
3. Anita Lasker-Wallfisch, *Inherit the Truth 1939–1945* (London: Giles de la Mare, 1996), pp. 94–5.

Chapter 1
British Soldiers Encounter Belsen

In what was an unusual development, the Belsen camp was officially surrendered to the British on 12 April 1945 as part of a local ceasefire; the British army entered the camp on 15 April. The exact circumstances leading up to the surrender of the camp are difficult to establish, and this is a subject worthy of further research. In the early months of 1945, Heinrich Himmler had been persuaded to take part in secret negotiations with the Red Cross and the neutral countries in order to salvage all he could for himself despite the increasing chaos in the camps.[1] With the knowledge that there had been an outbreak of typhus in Belsen, Kurt Becher, an aide to Himmler, visited the camp in 10 April 1945. The Allies were quickly approaching Bergen-Belsen and it was clear to the German command in the area that they could not afford to move the inmates away from the front and so expose German troops to the threat of disease. On the recommendation of Becher, Himmler gave the order that Belsen should be evacuated or destroyed, as had been the fate of other camps in previous months, but instead Becher handed it over intact to the advancing British.

On 12 April Colonel Schmidt, a German emissary, came through the British lines to declare the presence of a concentration camp at Belsen. Later that day an agreement was reached between the Chief of Staff, 1st Parachute Army, Military Commandant Bergen and the Chief of Staff, British VIII Army Corps. The Germans agreed to neutralize a zone of 8 kilometres by 6 kilometres around the camp and erect 'Danger – Typhus' notices and white flags at all road entrances to the area. Wehrmacht troops were to be allowed to return to German lines, while the Hungarian troops guarding the camp were to be placed at the disposal of the British forces.

The 29th Armoured Brigade, involved in fierce fighting around Bergen, were the first British troops to come across the Belsen camp. Led by Brigadier Roscoe Harvey, they arrived at the site in the morning of 15 April. Harvey was unable to stop at the camp, but he did send a tank and a few men led by Brigadier Daniell to have a brief look and report on what they found. It was not until the afternoon of 15 April that Lieutenant-Colonel

R. I. G. Taylor's 63rd Anti-Tank Regiment, Royal Artillery, became the official liberators of Belsen.

Many of the soldiers involved in the liberation had experienced the full horrors of war, and yet not a single individual was prepared for what they were to encounter at Belsen in April 1945. For numerous men and women the part they played in the relief of the camp proved to be a central milestone not only of the war, but also of their lives as a whole. In the accounts that follow in this chapter, the first men into the camp give powerful descriptions of the scene that was revealed and their own initial responses. As important eyewitnesses in an era before mass television ownership, they felt the burden of adequately describing what they saw in a way that would be understood and assimilated by people at home. Their words, the substance of army reports, private letters and newspaper articles, informed the world about the concentration camps. Powerful visual images also followed later in the form of newsreel footage.

As detailed in the following accounts, a most pressing task for the liberators after bringing food supplies into the camp was to bury the vast numbers of dead and control the spread of disease. The burial pits were dug by a British army bulldozer and the Hungarian guards. SS personnel, with the exception of the camp commandant Josef Kramer, who was imprisoned in Celle on 18 April, were forced to do the burial work under the watchful eyes of survivors. Apparently, these guards were given the same rations as the inmates before release and were worked to exhaustion. The logistical and sanitary demands of the situation, however, required more radical methods. Hence the bulldozer was used to shove tangles of bodies directly into the pits, providing one of the most enduring and haunting images of mass, dehumanized mortality to emerge from the visual record of the Holocaust.

*

By means of hostages, the Germans intimated to us that there was within their lines a concentration camp containing 1,500 cases of Typhus but at no time did they give any indication of the appalling conditions we were to find there when we captured the area. As events proved, there must have been between 10,000 and 20,000 cases there.

[...]

Two British officers went over to the German lines to discuss how the situation could best be dealt with. The Germans were asked to give up the whole area but they naturally pointed out that this would turn the whole of their defensive position on the right flank; it was therefore agreed that no troops should be deployed within the camp perimeter and that no artillery fire should be directed into or from the area. The German commander was to ensure that all SS, except those required for administration, should leave the camp before the arrival of any British force; those required must be disarmed and would become prisoners. A battalion of Wehrmacht was to be kept to act as guards and prevent the escape into the surrounding country of any internees who might be infectious but as soon as the British forces could take over this duty the Wehrmacht would be given safe conduct back to the German lines.

Although it would be the Eleventh Armoured Division which would capture the area, it was evident that the control and cleaning of the area would become a 'Second Army' problem. At the time we were still fighting hard; it was indeed one of the most important periods of the Campaign because we had got the German Army on the run; as a result every British division was heavily engaged.

The demands on our own Medical Services at that time were very great with fighting commitments alone but in addition there were vast numbers of displaced persons streaming back and also large collections of German wounded in the many hospitals, both military and civil, on the line of our advance, both heavy medical commitments. The medical units available were therefore very few and all that could be spared initially was one Casualty Clearing Station, one Light Field Ambulance and two Field Hygiene Sections.

Brigadier H. L. Glyn-Hughes, *RAMC, DDMS 2nd Army, BLA*[2]

I think that for quite a long time no food or fuel had been delivered at the Camp, so the Commandant, Colonel Kramer, had just left them to die of slow starvation, and various diseases. This was all the more ghastly as Belsen Camp was situated in part of the most fertile farmland in Germany, abounding in cabbages, potatoes, beans and wheat, yet not a cartload was delivered to the Camp, or a single pig or chicken. [Brigadier] Roscoe Harvey asked me how many of the thousand or so inmates I thought would recover with good medical care. I replied maybe six or a dozen.

Brigadier R. B. T. Daniell DSO, *Commanding Officer, 13 Regiment,*
Honourable Artillery Company, Royal Horse Artillery[3]

I knew no more than someone had found a concentration camp and that they thought there was typhus in it. The first indication I had that we were arriving at our destination was when we passed the huge Wehrmacht Cavalry Barracks. One learns in war to be surprised at nothing but when we passed German guards, SS men strolling about fully armed and groups of immaculate German officers all of whom were punctilious with their salutes, I realised we were in for an odd party. We chose a site to establish our camp in a remarkably clean, fresh field amid beautiful wooded country with no sign of Belsen, the barracks or in fact any evidence of German occupation. Apart from the guns and the smoke from burning buildings in the distance we might have been a dozen miles from the war and not right in the middle of it.

Lieutenant-Colonel M. W. Gonin, Commanding Officer,
11 Light Field Ambulance, RAMC[4]

We drove through the SS compound and stationed our loud-hailer car outside the wire gate leading into the inmates' camp. Beaming the loud-speakers in the direction of the camp we said, first in German, then in French:

> The Germans have nothing more to do with this camp. The camp is now under control of the British Army. Food and medical aid are being rushed up immediately. Obey our orders and instructions. By so doing you will help us and it is the best way by which you can help yourselves.

Following Brigadier Hughes and Colonel Taylor in their jeeps we drove right through the camp, stationed ourselves near the crematorium at the far end, and made the same loud-speaker announcement. It must have been audible everywhere, and it was the beginning of the appeal to reason instead of fear, of the use of the human voice in place of the rifle and the truncheon.

Derrick Sington, Commander of 14 Amplifier Unit, Intelligence Corps[5]

The extent of the problem had not really been fully relayed – and had probably not been fully known – but we certainly were not told. It was quite an unexpected sight that we met. It was dark, and we came in and settled down for the night, and the extent of what was before us came to light in the morning [...]

The only way really to describe it is the fact that there was just a carpet of human bodies, mostly very emaciated, many of them unclothed, jumbled together; people had just died where they stood. And they were outside, and inside, the various huts. Outside, lying where there were any trees or any open ground, it was incredible: the mass of bodies that didn't putrefy because they were so skeletal – there was so little flesh on them: their arms and their legs were just like matchsticks really. It was a gruesome and horrible sight that I will never forget, never.

Major Alexander Smith Allan, 113 Light Anti-Aircraft Regiment[6]

It is quite impossible to give any adequate description on paper of the atrocious, horrible, and utterly inhumane condition of affairs.

The prisoners were a dense mass of emaciated apathetic scarecrows huddled together in wooden huts, and in many cases without beds and blankets, and in some cases without any clothing whatsoever. The females were in worse condition than the men and their clothing generally, if they had any, only filthy rags.

The dead lay all over the Camp and in piles outside the blocks of huts, which housed the worst of the sick and were miscalled hospitals. There were thousands of naked and emaciated corpses in various stages of decomposition lying about this Camp. As far as can be ascertained there were some 13,000 dead lying unburied.

Sanitation was to all practical purposes non-existent. Pits, with, in only a few instances, wooden perch rails, were available in totally inadequate numbers. The majority of inmates, from starvation, apathy and weakness, defecated and urinated where they sat or lay, even inside the living huts.

Ablution arrangements were completely inadequate. There was no running water or electricity. All water was brought in by British water trucks.

Lieutenant-Colonel James Alexander Deans Johnston,
32 (British) CCS[7]

Belsen, as we saw it on the day of its liberation, 15th April 1945, can be described as follows: Camp 1, referred to as the 'horror camp', contained 40,000 people, made up of approximately 28,000 women and 12,000 men.

At the entrance was an administrative area, where were situated offices, accommodation for guards, stores and prison cells. The camp proper was a heavily wired perimeter with guard towers spaced at regular intervals around it and from which for the first 48 hours continual shots were being fired. The perimeter enclosed five compounds, four on the left and one on the right of a broad road running through the camp. Three of these were for men and contained numbers varying from 1,500 to 8,000.

The two for women contained, the one on the left – 5,000 and the one on the right – 23,000. The whole camp was originally built to contain 8,000 and on our arrival were found 40,000 living, whilst on the ground were 10,000 corpses, and it was further reported that in addition 17,000 had died during the previous month of March.

After a quick survey of the whole camp area an appreciation was made that 25,000 required immediate hospitalisation and of this number 10,000 would probably die, despite all efforts. These figures proved to be very near the mark, although the number of deaths after liberation was higher, approximately 13,000.

In the camp there was no sign of hygiene at all, huts which should have contained at the most 80 to 100 prisoners, in some cases had as many as 1,000. Some huts had a lavatory but this had long ceased to function and the authorities had made no provision outside, so that conditions on the ground and in the huts themselves were appalling, especially when it is realised that starvation, diarrhoea and dysentery were rife.

Apart from the frightful conditions in compounds and huts there were many horrors – the enormous pile of dead lying everywhere, a crematorium, a gallows in the centre of the camp and signs of mass burial – one enormous grave open and half filled on our arrival.

That is a broad picture of Belsen. The magnitude of the task was not really apparent until one got into the huts and one was faced with the appalling stench and the sight of countless numbers of miserable skeletons herded together on the floor or in bunks, often four to a bed and the living sharing with the dead. In one hut were counted twenty women in 35 square feet; the bare minimum of space allotted to one British soldier in the most crowded conditions. There were few blankets and many were without clothing at all; there was no straw and few rooms had bunks.

Brigadier H. L. Glyn-Hughes

The only water available was from filthy static water tanks most of which contained a body or two when we arrived. The majority of the inmates had either had typhus or were suffering from it; most other diseases known to man, except cholera, were rife and practically all the internees were abnormal mentally. No human being, even if they were sane when admitted to the camp, and many were not, could remain in the horror camp and keep their sanity. The internees were eating the corpses of those who had died, the only eatable portions were the kidneys, livers and hearts.

Lieutenant-Colonel M. W. Gonin

Our job was to be a unique task for any medical unit – to treat the sick of a large concentration camp. That was all we were told. Vaguely interested, we proceeded. After passing by a notice reading 'Danger – Typhus', we entered a gate guarded by an armed man in a brown uniform. What I saw next was unforgettable. Hundreds upon hundreds of men, leaning out of windows and lining the streets, were cheering and waving. They were a pitiful sight, heads shaven, dressed in pyjama-like striped garments – they were thin, pallid, wretched. Russians, French, Italians, Yugoslavs, Poles, Norwegians – all the nationalities on earth seemed to be represented. We drove on, turned into a field nearby, unloaded the lorries and began pitching our tents. Soon the whisper went round – 'This camp is worse than anything we have read about. 60,000 people are in it. All are undernourished, 15,000 have typhus or dysentry; hundreds are dying every week. Corpses lie about everywhere – the stench is awful.'

The next morning (17 April '45) on parade, our O.C. addressed us. He had visited the 'horror camp' and corroborated the rumours. 'It is unbelievable' he said, 'there is no organisation, no food, nothing. Half-starved, emaciated, spiritless, demented, these people roaming the camp have been reduced to animal level. I went through the womens' quarter of the camp hospital. Many of them are stark naked and are literally crawling about on their hands and knees, too weak to walk. The bedridden, just skin and bone, lie in their own dung. In one small room were forty women, few with any clothes, huddled together to keep warm. Some of these women had been dead for days – nobody had come to dispose of their bodies. I have seen some sights, I thought I could take anything – but this "shook" me, made me want to vomit. Outside, the dead are piled four feet high over a large area and bulldozers are having to be employed to shovel the bodies into large pits. I could tell you more, even worse, but it's too sickening to talk about.'

[...]

This evening my friend and I managed to slip into the horror camp in an army lorry. We saw only a part of it and we were assured that conditions were seventy-five per cent better than yesterday. What my informant meant was that a large proportion of the dead had been buried, and that the smell of the camp was a little improved. Words cannot adequately describe what I saw. The prisoners' quarters were shacks, bounded by barbed wire. Outside, these pitiful wrecks walked about, enjoying the freedom of movement. Never have I seen men and women so thin. 'Shrunken eyes, pallid complexion, skin and bone,' would fully describe most of them. [...]

Private Emmanuel Fisher, *32 Casualty Clearing Station, RAMC, BLA*[8]

At approximately 1800 hours on the afternoon of 15th April 1945 I was interrogating Josef Kramer, Commandant of Belsen Camp [...] At about this time a runner came to report shooting by SS Guards at the Western end of the Men's Camp. I proceeded immediately to the spot in company with Lieutenant-Colonel Taylor, taking Josef Kramer with us.

At the Western end of the Men's Camp, some thirty yards due east of the gate leading thence to the crematorium, I found a stack of straw covered potato plants. A number of male internees of the Camp were foraging in the stack for food. Surrounding them were three or four individual members of the SS Guards of the Camp armed with automatic weapons of Sten Gun type. As I approached the spot I saw and heard them firing single shots at the aforesaid internees and they made no attempt to cease firing when I came up to them, Josef Kramer made no attempt to prevent them or to interfere.

Such firing was indiscriminate and gave the impression of being a customary pastime. Several dead and dying internees were lying on and around the potato stack. I saw one or two fall as a result of the firing as I approached. [...]

We gave immediate orders to Kramer that all shooting at internees was to cease immediately, and that any further case reported to us would result in one SS Guard being shot for every internee killed. I also directed that the dead and wounded be removed for burial and medical attention respectively. At least one of the dead was carried away on my orders by Josef Kramer, who showed the utmost reluctance to comply with the order.

Despite my orders single shots were to be heard around the perimeter of the Camp, some of which may have come from the Guard towers, during the next 16 to 18 hours.

I formed the strongest impression that such shooting at internees was a popular sport among the Guards for no adequate reason since I am convinced that no attempts to escape were made after the British occupation commenced. A further repetition of orders to shoot one for one was necessary before this could finally be stopped.

On the 16th April 1945 it was reported to me that some of the Hungarian soldiers employed as guards by the SS had broken into and looted the food stores. It was further reported that food sent by charitable organisations, principally Jewish, for the use of internees, was customarily regarded as the perquisite of the guards. I issued stringent orders to the Hungarians in this regard and no further such looting was reported.

Brigadier H. L. Glyn-Hughes, *PRO WO235/24*

The first person I arrested was Josef Kramer, the Camp Commandant, known as the Beast of Belsen. On the day our unit arrived, I locked Kramer in a huge meat refrigerator set at a low temperature, which the Germans had been using for their own food supplies. I put two guards on him. He was in there for 24 hours before we took him out. Then I interrogated him and made out the arrest warrant.

[. . .]

I was very proud of being a Jew who arrested one of the most notorious gangsters in Nazi Germany. Maybe it was Fate that a Jew should arrest one of the war's worst concentration camp guards. It was a remarkable moment, but first and foremost I was doing my duty as a soldier, a British soldier, and these were evil men and women who had to be brought to justice.

Kramer was unshaven and very well-fed. He had a faraway look, like a frightened animal that's just been cornered. When I said: '*Look* at these people . . . ' he shrugged his shoulders and said: 'We had no medical supplies, and not enough food for ourselves.' I said: 'Look at *you*! You look as if you ate enough for three people.' He kept mumbling to himself: 'I only acted on orders from my superiors.' But he was the camp commandant!

[. . .]

This was civilisation at its lowest point. It is not humanly possible to believe that anyone can carry out such atrocities and be totally without pity.

There was no opposition from the SS. They gave us no trouble whatsoever. Not one of them tried to fight back, because they were cowards. They only felt themselves brave when they were dealing with unarmed men, women, children and babies. Then they felt superior, but when faced with armies and soldiers they felt small and dejected.

The SS women were the same. They were silent and there was no conversation among them. They looked neither happy nor sad. It was as if they had been drugged.

[. . .]

We made the SS shift all the bodies into huge pits or craters which were dug by bulldozers. There were thousands of bodies: poor, innocent ex-people, human beings. The SS had to handle them, load the skeletons on to lorries, take the lorries up to the pits and throw the bodies inside. Then the bulldozers filled in this mass grave.

After supervising this for a day or two, our soldiers had become so embittered at what they had seen that, when some of the SS tried to run away, they (the British) emptied their machine guns into them. These boys were so shocked that I think they would have killed any German they had come across.

At first there were 160 SS, but half of them escaped into the forest behind the camp. The agreement with the Wehrmacht was for the Wehrmacht soldiers to go back behind the German lines once the British had taken over the camp, only on condition that the SS remained. The Dutch Resistance fighters who had joined the British Army after Holland had been liberated were waiting for them in the forest and strung them up. The 80 or so SS remaining in the camp knew that the war was over for them.

Some committed suicide. When we put them in the cells we left pieces of rope around and some hanged themselves. They knew they would have no chance, because their crimes were so great.

[. . .]

On April 18, three days after our arrival, I woke up and could not get out of bed. I was paralysed. That happened to two or three of our chaps. We simply could not walk. When the doctor came and stuck pins in our legs, we felt nothing. This lasted for 24 hours, and they put it down to shock on our nerves from the horrific sights we'd seen.

Sergeant Norman Turgel, *53 Field Security Section,*
British Intelligence Corps[9]

[. . .] I and my Second in Command went to the Horror Camp to get some idea of the problems we were up against when we came to move the inmates. I can give no adequate description of the Horror Camp in which my men and myself were to spend the next month of our lives. It was just a barren wilderness, as bare and devoid of vegetation as a chicken run. Corpses lay everywhere, some in huge piles where they had been dumped by other inmates, sometimes they lay singly or in pairs where they had fallen as they shuffled along the dirt tracks. Those who died of disease usually died in the huts, when starvation was the chief cause of death they died in the open for it is an odd characteristic of starvation that its victims seem compelled to go on wandering till they fall down and die. Once they have fallen they die almost at once and it took a little time to get used to seeing men, women and children collapse as you walked by them and to restrain oneself from going to their assistance. One had to get used early to the idea that the individual just did not count. One knew that five hundred a day were dying and that five hundred a day were going [to go] on dying for weeks before anything we could do would have the slightest effect. It was, however, not easy to watch a child choking to death from diphtheria when you knew a tracheotomy and nursing would save it. One saw women drowning in their own vomit because they were too weak to turn over, and men eating worms as they clutched half a loaf of bread purely because they had had to eat worms to live and now could scarcely tell the difference between worms and bread.

Piles of corpses, naked and obscene, with a woman too weak to stand, propping herself against them as she cooked the food we had given her over an open fire; men and women crouching down just anywhere in the open, relieving themselves of the dysentery which was scouring their bowels; a woman standing stark naked washing herself with some issue soap in water from a tank in which the remains of a child floated.

[...]

I stood there looking round in this silence of death. Suddenly someone noticed my red cross armband and cried, 'Docteur Engleesh docteur'. There was an instant response of weak little cries of joy, feeble clapping, or just weak grunts of greeting. One girl was too weak to clap or even to speak, she just smiled – it was the most wonderful smile I have ever seen and worth all the horrors of Belsen. When I next went there she had joined the pile of corpses. One was very proud at that moment of being British and being a doctor but it gave birth to a hatred of the German of which at times I am almost frightened. I took a British Brigadier with three DSOs into that hut two days later and when he left it he was crying like a child.

I will take you into hut 302. This is not a hospital hut but an ordinary living hut. A central corridor with two rooms some sixty yards long, I measured it carefully. It would have held, by British army standards, 83 soldiers – we removed from it 1,426 women and that does not count the dead. Starvation without typhus or dysentery produces the most appalling diarrhoea. No inmate was allowed out of that hut after six o'clock at night, there was one lavatory. One had to wear rubber boots – the floor was thick with faeces. The hut was raised a couple of feet above ground level, most of the flooring in the corridor had been pulled up and the space beneath used as a latrine and contained in addition many corpses. March is cold in Germany, there was no [heating] and few of the internees had any clothing at all. If one died the poor wretch crouching next to the body would crawl on top of it for the sake of a brief spell of warmth. They all had typhus as well as many other diseases such as TB, *cancrum oris*, in which the flesh of the face rots away, syphilis, fractures in which the bones protruded through the gangrenous flesh. When one went in they screamed at one in a dozen different languages crying to be taken away, praying not to be sent to 'the gas' or to 'the fire'.

Lieutenant-Colonel M. W. Gonin

I don't know whether it was the fact that they were so spare and lean – it was a very unpleasant smell, but not so much as one would expect. I've smelt worse in Normandy, through killed cows and so on lying in fields, getting putrescent and so on. Inside the huts of course, it was appalling, because not only were there the living – who could hardly do anything, could hardly move or do anything for themselves – but of course there were bodies inside as well. So the big thing was that we had to do something about the bodies and remove them and give them some burial. And it was impossible to do anything except bury them in mass pits. And of course the ground was rather sandy there. Bulldozers were very little use because the soil was so sandy (even when it was wet down to try to get bulldozed) so shovelling had to be done. That was done by the large Hungarian force of troops left there, who had been prison guards: they were given shovels and they had to dig pits, and into these pits the bodies were gradually put. I think a pretty good estimate is that there were over 10,000 corpses to bury. [. . .] German troops were used and the SS were used sometimes for this, the British soldiers in a supervisory capacity all the time, watching the pits being gradually filled up. And when they were filled up, earth was spread over the top, put down about 2ft high, and a notice was put up with the date and approximate number of bodies. Eventually, after the big burial got reduced, we were able to have individual burials.

Major Alexander Smith Allan

S.S. men are being made to load the bodies on to trucks for transportation to the pits. [. . .] The scene was circled by the internees – to them the scene was terribly funny – they jeered and laughed when one guard fell over a corpse.

A child – she couldn't have been more than ten years of age came up to me with a beaming face – she watched what was happening for a few moments. Then said to me with the same beaming face, 'That is good'. A child of that age – who shouldn't have seen a corpse – that she should be able to look at a pile of starved bodies being manhandled onto lorries and find amusement in it! She was completely unmoved by death and filth. Of course, there were some very young children playing a few yards from this path – they've never known anything else.

There are no latrines – there never have been any. You come out of your hut and squat down by the side of the wall – no one pays any attention to you – man or woman. This doesn't help the smell around the place. If you want to strip off in public, no one will mind. Most people do it, for self-respect and decency are gone in the majority of cases. You do this, and then pick off the larger lice. They are reverting to animals.

If you are 'fit', you sleep in one of the ordinary bunks. There is no room to lie down. You sit with your knees apart, the person in front sits between them, and leans back on you, you do the same to the person behind; and the one at the back, leans on the wall.

From the internees' point of view, the highlight of the afternoon was the shooting of an S.S. guard – he tried to escape. They loved that. We wondered what all the cheering was about. They were in great glee when four other guards were made to load his body on a lorry. So, you see, the whole scale of life has changed; and death no longer means anything. It appears the guards had a choice game of shooting at the internees when they were defecating, their white bottoms made a good target.

[. . .] If only for this camp alone (to free it) – the war has been just and worthwhile; but there must be others like it and worse.

Sorry this is such a fearful letter, but you can't smell the place, if it's any consolation – I still can. You do realise that people at home must know of this and what they have missed. I heard that the average life of any person over 40 in the camp was one month.

Shall be much more cheerful after a night's sleep, but to-day has been like a madhouse – everything so incongruous.

Captain J. Gant, *21 Light Field Ambulance BLA*[10]

One could not go far into Belsen Camp without seeing a huge pile, or rather, a little mountain of boots and shoes. For years past every internee entering the camp had to give up a pair of boots or shoes. Even babies' shoes were plentiful. Gold and other valuables had once been found hidden in the soles of footwear. Henceforth a search was made for anything capable of being sewn up between the seams. The mound of leather was about 15ft high. Much of the older material had evidently been removed and probably used as fuel, but when an opportunity came their way the starving prisoners rummaged into the pile in search of something to wear, or to chew.

Reverend Father Edmund Swift, *Roman Catholic Chaplain to 81 British General Hospital*[11]

On the grass bordering the sidewalks, there are men and women apparently asleep, but not a few are dead. There are so many and nobody has time to move them. Beyond them, the bodies are in piles – there are hundreds of them

– naked, for the clothes are needed badly and a good pair of boots is hard to come by. The bodies are jumbled in a heap where they have been thrown. Some are blackening already and the stench is foul. This pile is not more than three yards from the path where the internees are laughing and talking. Where people step over dead and the half-dead, still in conversation, while smiling at our soldiers. There is a holiday atmosphere about – the internees are at last free from the guards and everyone is smiling and laughing. Some of the girls are well dressed and well-fed. Some, even, have silk stockings. It is assumed that these have only been in a few days.

Then you can see that there is starvation, thin arms and thin faces in others. People fall down and are unable to get up. They may be helped up or they may die there – they are mainly the older ones. The living have become horribly accustomed to the dead. It's then you realise that everything these people feel is varying on hysteria – it is hysteria.

The hospital is full. It's not a hospital, but a hut which has the luxury of having double-bunk barrack beds fitted. We went into the women's ward. The room, as was to be expected, was overcrowded. All the women were sitting up. They cheered and clapped their hands when we came in – of course you can't lie down when there are four of you in a single bed – especially the German Army pattern which is like a shallow wooden box. So they have their typhus, dysentery, typhoid, T.B. and other diseases in this position; and they die like that – which accounted for the large pile of corpses outside.

Captain J. Gant

The situation was comical in many ways. Everywhere were Germans and Hungarians armed with rifles and hand grenades. The territory was in fact neutral; thus the guard on the gates consisted of our own 'Red-Caps' (Military Police) and Germans or Hungarians; and it was quite a common sight to see an armed Nazi walking out with his wife or best girl. This morning however (19th) I witnessed the fulfilment of the truce. Eight hundred Jerry infantrymen and their officers formed a half square just a hundred yards from my tent. They were packed and ready to go. British high-ranking officers were conversing with them through a Belgian interpreter. Soon five mobile Bofors guns rolled up and the crews, immediately on halting, trained their guns on the Jerries. An artillery officer quickly ordered the guns to be pointed in a different direction. The Jerry officers (one was almost the double of Erich von Stroheim as Rommel in the film 'Five Graves to Cairo') parlayed with the British. Then one of them addressed his men through a loud speaker, commencing 'My soldiers' and going on to explain (as if they didn't already know) that the time had come for them to go back. He expected absolute obedience to enable the conditions of the truce to be fulfilled. I stood there with my friend and our Nursing Officers and smiled at the thought of all those Jerries going back. Of the eight hundred, only thirty-five wanted to return to their lines.

Emmanuel Fisher

S/325458
Sister K. J. Elvidge
QAIMNS/R
29th BGH
BLA

26.5.45

My Darling,

Another letter from you today, it's good to have them, they help tremendously, especially here, where we seem to be more or less cut off from the rest of the world.

All that you have heard and read in the newspapers of this place is perfectly true and in some cases even worse. It is absolutely incredible that human beings could sink so low as to treat fellow human beings as they have been treated in this camp.

The whole camp is divided up now into smaller camps. The whole thing itself is about 25 miles square. No. 1 Camp, the 'horror camp', was burnt down a few days before we arrived and the inmates transferred to hospital which now comprises Camp Two. This is made up of Barrack Squares, which were occupied by the German SS Troops. Each Square consists of five blocks, each of which hold 150 patients, and a Sister is in charge of each. The 9th BGH is also here and between us we have about 13,000 patients. They are only half our size, so we have two-thirds and they have the remainder.

There are two other camps, 3 and 4 which are transit camps, the patients are transferred there from hospital as soon as they are fit to travel, and there they await transfer to their own countries as soon as it can be arranged. This sounds quite a simple procedure, but believe me it is far from it. I could not attempt to explain the difficulties. The chief one is that of languages. The majority of the patients have some Jewish origin, but are from all countries under the sun. Russia, Poland, Hungary, Czheckoslovakia, Belgium, Holland, France, and only about four of them have a smattering of English. I have a staff comprising of one English VAD nurse, and then there are Polish nurses, Russian nurses, Hungarian soldiers to do the cleaning and German nurses who are on night duty. Out of that crowd, only one Polish nurse speaks English and that not very fluently. All the nurses themselves have been internees in various camps. There is one English doctor to each square of five blocks, so as you can imagine we don't see much of her. Then we have some Belgian medical students who also help, I've got two assigned to my block, and thank goodness, one of those speak very good English.

When the fighting got near Belsen, the Germans asked the British to take it over, as they said it had got out of hand. When the British did so, they found the place in a terrible state. There were about 21,000 housed in huts in the Camp proper (The horror Camp No. 1). About 1,000 were put in a hut which should normally hold about fifty. 500 or more died or were shot each day. They had various methods of getting rid of them. The kindest was shooting. They were all starved, and diseases such as TB, Typhus, dysentery etc. were absolutely rampant. A small forward hospital and some British troops moved in and they have done an amazing amount of work in the five weeks since it was liberated, but there is still such a lot to be done, it seems a hopeless task, but we shall just have to do our best, and make what we can of it.

I don't know whether you read this fact in the papers or not, but it is perfectly true, when the British entered the Camp, there were 10,000 dead lying about in piles, and those who were still alive used the dead bodies as pillows.

To come back to a more pleasant subject. You say that your leave is due July 5th. If you will apply for me to the war office and I will apply at this end, and surely surely, darling, I shall get it this time. I am just living for it.

All my love is yours dearest.

Kath

Sister K. J. Elvidge, letter dated 26 May 1945, IWM DD 89/10/1

NOTES

1. See Chapter 8 for a history of the camp system.
2. From a speech given at the Inter-Allied Conference, June 1945; Imperial War Museum, Department of Documents (hereafter IWM DD) and the Wellcome Archive, London.
3. IWM DD 85/9/1.
4. IWM DD 85/38/1.
5. *Belsen Uncovered* (London: Duckworth, 1946), p. 27.
6. IWM Sound Archive 11903/2.
7. Public Records Office, WO 235/24.
8. IWM DD 95/2/1.
9. From Gena Turgel, *I Light a Candle* (London: Vallentine Mitchell, 1995), pp.106–10.
10. IWM DD 99/82/1, from letter dated 18 April 1945.
11. IWM DD 90/4/1.

Chapter 2
Emergency Relief Measures in the Belsen Camp

Once the Wehrmacht troops stationed near the Belsen camp had returned to the German lines, the British were able fully to requisition the brick-built barracks complex, equipped with officers' mess and military hospital. Situated just a few kilometres from the main Belsen site, this accommodation proved to be the British army's main weapon in fighting to keep the Belsen inmates alive. Here they established what were designated as Camps 3 and 4, vast hospital areas where the former prisoners could be better treated (Camp 1 was the main 'horror camp' and Camp 2 the area of the barracks that had already been employed as an overflow camp by the SS administration before 15 April, holding 15,000 male prisoners).

The relief operation was led by Brigadier Glyn-Hughes, Deputy Director Medical Services, Second Army, who had visited the camp at an early stage on 15 April. With officers of the Royal Army Medical Corps, working under immense pressure and with few resources immediately available, he was forced to establish painful priorities. It was immediately apparent that the relief operation would be unable to save the whole camp population and that difficult decisions needed to be made in order to save anyone at all.

The logistics of a relief operation involving so many people were difficult enough but, in addition, the conditions in the camp were so monstrous as to turn even the most simple practical tasks into a terrible ordeal. The operation was split into two halves. The hospital areas were to be cleaned, equipped and prepared to take patients by 32 Casualty Clearing Station, while in the main camp, interim feeding stations were improvised and the dead buried under the direction of No. 10 Garrison Detachment and with the aid of 113 Light Anti-Aircraft Regiment.

The official British estimate of dead at the time of liberation was 10,000. It was not until 28 April that these were all buried. In addition, approximately 500 people died each day in the immediate aftermath of liberation, putting huge pressure on the delicate new infrastructure.

Although mass burials had already been going on for a week before 24 April, only at that time, after food and water supplies had been improved, did the British begin to keep anything approximating proper records of the burials. In the first instance signs were posted with estimates of the dead buried in each mass grave, and the date of burial; at these mass interments, a variety of clergymen of different faiths officiated. Later, the dead were buried individually, with the greatest level of identification possible.

30 Field Hygiene Section was charged with probably the largest single problem that British forces faced: containing and combating the epidemic form of typhus (*Fleckfieber*) that the SS had done virtually nothing to prevent. This dreadful disease more than any other was responsible for taking lives in Belsen, not only the lives of former internees but also those of the army personnel and the German medical workers drafted into the camp. The disease, spread by lice, killed within 24 hours of contraction and, if unchecked, could be expected to yield a 60 per cent mortality rate. As Paul Kemp points out, the epidemics that occurred in the camps were the last such instances in human history, with the potency of the disease greatly diminished towards the end of the 1940s by the introduction of broad-spectrum antibiotics.[1]

On 17 April, a medical conference established the fight against typhus as the main priority and on the next day 500 typhus patients were taken to the improvised military hospital in the Wehrmacht barracks. On 24 April the wholesale evacuation of the camp began. The typhus-infested huts were demolished as soon as they were empty, and anyone entering the camp was dusted with DDT powder.

Before large numbers of patients could be moved from the main camp, army units had to source practically everything they needed from the local population, including food and clothing, beds and bedding, and drugs and dressings – a huge project in itself. 'My own lorries got over 250 tons of medical equipment into the hospital area in the first week because I told my transport Sgt, "We must have medical supplies, for God's sake get them",' wrote Lieutenant-Colonel Gonin, whose detailed account is given here. Once the hospital areas were ready, a whole week into the operation, 11th Light Field Ambulance began the heartbreaking task of choosing who could be taken first from the filthy huts in Camp 1 to be nursed (among others, by six detachments of the British Red Cross) and so stand a chance of survival. Medical officers made swift, almost arbitrary decisions about priority in the evacuations. The inmates selected were stripped and taken in blankets by ambulance to the 'Human Laundry', sited in the erstwhile barrack stables. With the help of German nurses, these survivors were shaved and washed, treated with DDT and taken on to the hospital. With the ongoing evacuation process, death rates gradually declined. By 11 May, it was under a hundred a day.

The accounts of the early medical relief operation given below, in their immediacy and their detail, give us a powerful glimpse into the outlandish, frantic world that was Belsen in the final weeks of the war, 'the place of unending drama', to quote Gonin again. The entire operation was improvised and every imaginable obstacle was encountered and overcome.

Some of these obstacles were stark reminders of the realities of war – for example, when the retreating German officers sabotaged the water supply in the former barracks, so crucially delaying the relief effort, or when clearly marked ambulances were targeted by a German bomber. Others, by far the more numerous, were concerned with human encounters: the lack of a shared language; the mental state of the prisoners; the exhaustion of the medical teams; and animosity between people of different nationalities, both internees and relief workers.

It was not until 19 May, over four weeks after the British began to implement their relief strategy, that the last patients left Camp 1. Throughout this long month, the soldiers and medics were constantly surrounded and preoccupied by the dead and dying, all the time painfully aware that they were powerless to help fight the long-term effects of starvation and disease. 'To have attempted to save these men,' wrote Derrick Sington, 'to have tried to feed them one by one, even to ask their names, would have necessitated at least ten times the relief workers that were actually present at Belsen in those first few days.'

The last hut in the now completely empty camp barracks was ceremoniously burned down on 21 May. The British left only an entrance sign at the gates, which read:

This is the site of the infamous Belsen Concentration Camp
Liberated by the British on April 15, 1945
Ten thousand unburied dead were found here
Another thirteen thousand more have since died
All of them victims of the German New Order in Europe
And an example of Nazi Kultur

While certainly adjudged to be a necessary measure to prevent the spread of typhus, the burning of the barracks also had unforeseen consequences for some Belsen survivors. When returning to the place of the camp in later life, these survivors felt and still feel that they do not have a proper physical site on which to centre their memories of suffering beyond the mass graves, which are all that remain.

*

The problems were:

1. To stop the typhus spreading.
2. To bury the dead before the hot summer started cholera.
3. To feed the sick in the Horror Camp who were dying of starvation more rapidly than of their illness.
4. To remove from the Horror Camp those who might live with some form of systemized feeding and nursing.

5. To help those who lived to regain their humanity.

Lieutenant-Colonel M. W. Gonin, Commanding Officer,
11 Light Field Ambulance, RAMC[2]

The task of cleansing the area seemed at first insuperable and the first essential was supervision by more troops, particularly directed to administration.

What were we to do straightaway? It was first decided to give the best chance of survival to the greatest number and therefore to move out at once into the Barrack area the supposedly fit and well thereby making more room in the huts and supervision of feeding easier.

For many reasons it was not possible to implement these ideals in full which included the careful selection of the next cases to be moved in order of priority and it eventually came to a question of evacuating hut by hut.

The fact that there was a good barrack area which could be converted into a hospital undoubtedly saved the situation and, in addition, adjoining this area, was a beautiful military hospital of 500 beds and a large officers' mess in which the dining room alone could take 200 beds.

The main difficulty of course was equipment for the barrack area and it was obvious that this could not come from British Army sources in the number required. Eventually 14,000 beds were equipped from every conceivable source by combing out to a very wide area of country.

Brigadier H. L. Glyn-Hughes, RAMC, DDMS 2nd Army, BLA[3]

Once we'd run out of blankets and it looked as if evacuation from the Horror Camp might be held up for a day. Hughie [Brigadier Glyn Hughes] arrived and heard the difficulty. 'What's the population of Celle?' he asked. On being told 1,600 to what appeared an irrelevant question he said, 'Go to the Bürgermeister [Mayor] and say that I order that each civilian in Celle will hand in one blanket by midday tomorrow'. We got 1,800 blankets the following night.

Hughie was one of those men, like Churchill, that Britain produces in times of crises, without them we should never win through as we do. As soon as the time of peril is over they fade into the background and their places are taken by little men which I suppose is why we make such a horrid mess of our peace time affairs.

Lieutenant-Colonel M. W. Gonin

[Typhus is a disease] which is almost always fatal to the uninoculated over 40 years of age. It is an agonisingly painful disease characterised by intense thirst and headache until the patient reaches the typhus state which is a form of coma seen only in this disease. You can therefore appreciate some very small part of the agony these patients went through shut in huts. [. . .]

Typhus is produced by an infected louse. The louse lives on human blood and it is only the faeces of the infected louse which gets into the bloodstream of the patient through the puncture wound of the hungry louse that causes the disease. It can, however, also be contracted by breathing into the lungs dust consisting of the louse faeces. It was by this method that the men of my unit caught the disease after working in the horror camp.

Lieutenant-Colonel M. W. Gonin

The drill settled at [the] night's conference was that my unit [11th Light Field Ambulance] would move the sick from the Horror Camp. We should try and feed the sick in the Horror Camp until they could be moved. I should be responsible for the supply of medical equipment in the hospital area and I would arrange to remove the bodies of those who died in the hospital area. The MOs, nurses and orderlies of 32 CCS [Casualty Clearing Station] would be responsible for the care of the sick when they were in the hospital area with the help of any internee doctors and nurses we could produce from the Horror Camp.

All patients would be taken from the Horror Camp completely naked and wrapped in blankets. They would then go straight to what we called the Human Laundry where they would be washed, shaved and dusted by nurses from the German Military Hospital and then removed still naked to the wards in the hospital area. There they remained, still naked, until they died or we managed to clothe them.

Before any attempt could be made to move a single patient from the Horror Camp accommodation had to be prepared for them in the Hospital Area [...] 32 CCS got on with the job of cleaning up the filthy barrack rooms with the assistance of the Hungarians whom we found to be fairly willing workers once they understood who was their boss.

[...] These evening conferences became one of the features of Belsen. We met every evening at nine o'clock to discuss the difficulties, which at times seemed insurmountable, which had arisen during the day. Some twenty officers, three or four nursing sisters, Red Cross workers, St John's members, UNR[R]A would collect. The problems particular to the ladies would be discussed first, about eleven o'clock they would be dismissed, gin, brandy and champagne would appear and we would finish our business by twelve or one in the morning – and it was not a party but damned hard work which those meetings produced. I am very certain that it was the very considerable quantities of liquor that we got through at those meetings that kept those of us who were responsible for the administration of the place from going as mad as most of the internees in the Horror Camp.

[...]

Having carried out my recce [the day after his arrival and following the first conference] I decided we would evacuate first those women suffering from typhus and would disregard any other complaint which they might be suffering from in addition. In each larger [hut] we detailed one internee nurse or doctor to prepare a numerical roll of the number in each hut who was suffering from typhus and who was not most certainly going to die and they we decided to move first. On paper this method should have worked: it would have cleared the women's camp of typhus – it is nursing and only nursing that saves typhus lives – the typhus patients were in the greatest pain. It was quite obvious that the people in the hospital area would be greatly helped in both diagnosis and treatment if they could fill one ward completely with patients suffering from the same disease. We tried this for the first day but the system broke down. It was the human element that failed us; if the doctor or nurse in a particular hut was Polish then all the Poles were suffering from typhus and could be saved, if the nurse was Czech then all the Czechs were suffering from typhus and so on.

The day fixed to begin evacuation was dependent on when the chaps of 32 CCS were able to get a ward or block or square ready for patients. After many maddening delays owing to snags which were no one's fault zero day was fixed for April 22nd and on that morning all my ambulances were ready to move off at 7.30 a.m. [. . .] At 7.25 a.m. I received a message that the water supply in the hospital area had been sabotaged and no evacuation would be possible. This was a ghastly disappointment to us all. For five days we had been working in the Horror Camp feeding and doing what we could and all the time promising that the move would start as soon as possible, eventually we had been able to give the actual day. Morale in the camp rose a thousand per cent when the British arrived and food appeared. It began to fall when day after day passed and no one was moved. Of course the inmates could not realise the stupendous difficulties we were up against getting a place ready for them but having said we would start moving on a certain date and then not being able to do so was a frightful blow.

At this stage it was morale that was keeping people alive and nothing else. If they saw we did not keep our word they just lost again the will to live. I went to the poor expedient of sending my ambulances into the camp, letting them drive round and come out empty. We did not lift a patient but the word went round the camp that the ambulances had come. No one knew that they left, as they arrived, empty.

Two days later we did start and on the first day moved 720 patients to the hospital area. The routine we worked out was as follows: My ambulances were divided into two squads of ten cars in each squad, each squad had one MO and fifteen bearers. Each squad took a different hut so arranged that the traffic circuits did not interfere with each other. The MO went into each hut and marked on the forehead of each patient a cross to indicate to the bearers that this patient would be moved. [...] It was a heart-rending job and amounted to telling hundreds of poor wretches that they were being left to die. But as I have said the individual did not count. No one except myself knows what those MOs and stretcher-bearers [went through], many of the latter were youngsters who had experienced nothing except the clean deaths of battle. They were magnificent. They spent from 8 a.m. to 5 p.m., with an hour for lunch in those huts in the worst stench in the world, the stink of the unwashed living with every disease of God's earth mixed with that of the long unburied dead. They had to strip those living corpses of their rags, wrap them in blankets and carry them to the ambulance cars. They had to use brute force to prevent the more or less well from fighting their way onto the vehicles and to argue with excitable and half crazy central European doctors as to why their own particular friends could not be moved. Their pride in their job was terrific [...]. Sixty men including three officers of my unit worked in that camp and twenty one of them and one officer took ill with typhus before we had that camp clear.

When an ambulance was loaded it did the journey of two miles to the hospital area where it went to the Human Laundry. This was located in one of the cavalry stables, a long building capable of holding 150 horses. Here we had 60 tables at each of which worked two nurses from the German Military Hospital with two German MOs in charge under the pathologist of 32 CCS. [...]

The German nurses were an interesting study. At the start they laughed, joked, were definitely truculent, made no effort to get things ready for the job in hand, damned if they were going to work for the something [*sic*; euphemism for expletive] British. And then the first patients started to arrive. I am told by my friend who was in charge of the laundry that this was one of the most dramatic moments at Belsen, the place of unending drama. Those nurses stood with their mouths open and gazed in horror as those bodies were brought in, first one then another started to sob until almost the whole sixty were weeping. There was no more truculence after that. Those girls worked like slaves, they went down with typhus and they died but others took their place. They grew thin and they grew pale but they worked and they toiled from eight in the morning till six at night. They earned our respect; in the end we gave them tea in the mid morning and cigarettes. I have no time to go into the psychology of the German tonight and will merely quote Sir William Gull, a famous physician of the XIX century who said, 'Nursing is sometimes a trade, it is sometimes a profession, it ought to be a religion'. I believe in their case it was.

Lieutenant-Colonel M. W. Gonin

Miss J Rudman
Physiotherapy Service
9th (Br.) General Hospital
B.L.A.

14.5.45.

My Dearest Bill,
[. . .]
You said you'd be interested to hear my views of the German people, well
you can guess what they are when I tell you that I saw the end of the war in
Belsen concentration camp, we have been here a fortnight and it's terrible,
for propaganda reasons I'm allowed to tell you just where we are and all
about it.

I never expected to be in such a place for V day, not that it meant much to
me, I never wanted to be in England for that and seeing the papers has made
me realise I couldn't have stood it. Only the King mentioned those who had
helped to make this victory possible and yet didn't live to see the day, people
forget so easily unless they've lost someone themselves. I felt very sad,
thought what this might have meant to me once, I'm glad it's over of course,
but didn't feel like rejoicing.

There was very little reaction here, an R.A. parade and a terrific firing of
guns, the usual parties with perhaps a few more drinks than usual.

I just wanted to be by myself and was glad everyone else went to a party.
Apart from my personal feelings one could hardly think of peace when there's
so much human misery as there is here.

The camp is situated in a huge pine forest 25 sq. miles in all. It was an S.S.
training camp and there were 70,000 internees altogether, mostly Jews or
political prisoners, many of them once very eminent men. These poor things
were herded together in what we call Camp 1, 400 at a time in huts big enough
to hold 40, there wasn't a latrine in the place, those that could crawled outside,
but hundreds couldn't, and in amongst all this filth, women even had their
babies. You can imagine the smell!! Even though we have cleaned it up an
awful lot, it's still terrible, I can't get rid of it, take it with me when I'm away
from the place, still seems to be there.

The whole place has been declared a typhus zone, we're alive with it, we
ourselves work with our hair completely covered and we spray ourselves with
de-lousing powder every night and have had injections, so should be alright.

There are 100 London medical students working in Camp 1, they sort out
the living from the dead and those they think most likely to recover are got
out first.

They are then sent to the human laundry, where they are literally scrubbed on tables, hair shaved if necessary and de-loused. We have put German nurses on this work, some have already got typhus. When I went along one afternoon, there were 50 naked women, so emaciated, you could have cut yourself on their ribs being scrubbed down by these German girls just as if they were a lot of cattle, there were men of every description, ambulance drivers, stretcher bearers etc, all walking in and out, but these poor things have been so humiliated the last few years, they thought nothing of this.

From the laundry they come to us. The hospital is in what was the barracks, squares and squares of them, we are to be responsible for 5,000 patients, there is also a C.C.S. here and 3 Field Ambulances and countless other non-medical units.

We don't do any treatments at all, as we have hundreds of German doctors and nurses working under our supervision and more are arriving daily.

Our main job is the feeding, a terrific problem, because all these people are starved. We have 3 diets for them, 1, 2 + 3 according to the state of their health, they all see the food and want it, but many are quite incapable of eating it. On the other hand when they are up and helping to look after the others they want much more than we can give them there are so many and they hang around all the garbage bins and eat anything. To save us going back to our camp, we have tea and sandwiches brought to the square every afternoon for all British personnel, it's terrible Bill, we are surrounded by hundreds of hungry inmates waiting for scraps, we daren't give anything to one, we'd be lynched by hundreds all wanting the same it's pathetic and the same with cig ends, they hang around waiting for you to throw your end away. I feel disgustingly healthy and think of all the meals I've turned down in my time.

We aren't doing any physiotherapy at all except sunlight for the babies, it's all we're allowed to do as the British aren't to do any treatments. […] The rest of our time we are in the hospital office dealing with bed states deaths etc, and enquiries. I quite like it really, we have all sorts of people in and out all day, have to have an interpreter, there are literally dozens of languages and you'd never believe the international crises that arise.

The children's ward would break your heart, tiny little scraps, 2 in a bed with 2 big eyes staring out of a sunken face and little babies just like birds. I want to cry every time I go near the place, to think that innocent little children should have suffered so much. Then there's the maternity block, babies born all the time, there are 40 due now, lots die although we fight to save them, God knows why, I can't think they'll ever be any good. Every inmate down to the smallest child was branded with a number.

These people have lost all their human instincts and become animals they perform their essentials wherever they happen to be, never will I forget this smell as long as I live.

The clothing is a great problem too can't get enough, lots only have a blanket and wander around in this, then if it's hot they just drop it off. They wander out and die by the roadside, I've already found 2 corpses much to my horror. The corpses are put in the cellars every night and collected by a cart commonly known as the corpse cart, which I always seem to be meeting this cart, but you can't imagine the corpses as ever having lived.

I hope to God we don't stay here long, it's such a thankless task, and such a colossal one, should think it would take months to clean the place up. I think I'd rather go to Burma than stay here, they are asking for volunteers for B[urma]. I shan't do that, but expect I shall end up there anyway.

We are living under canvas again in God's clean fresh air, it was very cold and wet when we first arrived but we've had a spell of lovely hot weather and I'd loved it, and under these conditions feel it's a much more healthy way of living.

There is quite a lot of social life inside the camp, parties etc, and there's also a cinema in what was the SS officers quarters, a wonderful place complete with ballroom, cocktail bar etc., they certainly did themselves well, the swine.

I've always hated the Germans in this war, but now that I've seen what they've done to these people I feel I'll hate them for ever, you'd never believe such cruelty would exist.

The Jerry doctors and nurses are really quite efficient, although lazy. We've put the SS to do all the menial tasks in Camp 1, and they are gradually dying off of typhus, they'll be killed in the end anyway. There were 30 SS women amongst them.

[...]

We had a lovely drive up here, took us 2 days, it was quite a thrill crossing the Rhine on the Roosevelt bridge. We stayed one night in Osnabrück, not much left of that, we were completely ignored by the civilians who just behaved as if the British weren't there at all.

I don't think the majority of Germans knew the atrocities that were going on in these sort of places, they knew there *were* concentration camps, but that's all.

[...]

Do write again soon, I need something for the old morale in this place,

Lots of love,

Ruddy.

Miss J. Rudman, *9th (Br) General Hospital, BLA*[4]

[In the main camp,] one of the biggest problems really was how to feed the rest of the inmates who were still alive. It was a vast job really, because there was no water supply as such, there was no food. We did get an awful lot of food from a Wehrmacht barracks – food stocks were uncovered there. We got a dump of tentage and we pitched that to relieve the overcrowding. We had about 10,000 (there were about 40–50,000 people) allocated to each cookhouse – and we had to adapt cookhouses, and erect cookhouses, and even build one from scratch. The RA [Royal Artillery] carpenters all chipped in – and anybody who knew anything about building – and up it went: we got a new cookhouse going. The only kind of food containers we had to issue food with were kind of dustbins really. I'm afraid in the original stages we probably didn't help people at all by the diet because it wasn't controlled and we didn't know what we were doing. It wasn't until we got help in from 2nd Army and we got diet experts in – Brigadier Glyn Hughes got them in [that] we had Bengal famine diet and so on which people were able to take. We had various grades of diet in each kitchen, about three grades for those who were weaker and so on. The amazing thing was – within two or three weeks – the difference: they looked like human beings, instead of living skeletons, they seemed to recover extremely well.

Major Alexander Smith Allan, *113 Light Anti-Aircraft Regiment*[5]

While we were evacuating the Horror Camp my RSM had taken on the task of feeding some of the sick. It was little he could do but by begging, borrowing and stealing food he and 8 men with him distributed 4,000 meals twice a day – a tremendous undertaking. The need of it was self evident. The Gunners were doing wonders in running a kitchen to which these internees who could walk would come with bins and collect food, hot soup etc., which they took back to the inmates of the huts where it was distributed. At least it got to those who were fit enough to come to the bins when they were brought to the huts. If they were too weak to go to the distributors, or if they were of the wrong nationality they got none. By the wrong nationality I mean that whatever nationality was in the majority in any hut they got the food. I believe there were exceptions, the Dutch and French would help people of other races but in most cases there was a most distressing racial feeling.

Lieutenant-Colonel M. W. Gonin

Some ten days after we had come to Belsen all my ambulances were drawn up in our nice clean field, in this neutral area of Belsen, thousands of yards from any possible military objective, at 7.30 in the morning waiting to start work. There was the noise of an unusual plane engine and the rattle of machine gun fire. I had just time to get under my caravan when the planes came back a second time. They machine gunned and cannoned our camp three times, killing one of my men and seriously wounding four others. Twenty ambulances, each with four large red crosses, a large red cross flag on the ground and a red cross flag flying below my Union Jack. One of the German M.O.s at the laundry could speak English and that morning I went to him in a fury (I was fairly near shooting the fellow with my revolver). I told him exactly what had happened and what I thought of him and everything German. 'I am so sorry, Sir', he said and tears ran down his cheeks. The pride of the German army was again hurt. There was a lot of crying at Belsen.

Lieutenant-Colonel M. W. Gonin

But let us walk through the camp. Those big signboards plastered on every corner say, in effect, 'The Enemy Hears You!' – perhaps you will have noticed on every door, window and telephone the notice 'Pst!' (PST!). I think you will agree that there was every need of secrecy before we finish this walk; for you must remember this is just the after-effect which we are witnessing.

What are those blankets stretched on the grass verge outside the hospital wards you want to know. You have seen over a dozen in just a brief walk. In case you have not guessed, those blankets enclose the remains of skeleton like creatures, which the best of medical treatment could not save. The 'death wagon' will be along in a minute so let's get somewhere else. Let us go back to the better part of the camp. The DPs (displaced persons) are about now on their way to get some potatoes, although it looks more like a prossession to a maternity home. Look at that girl barely fourteen, and that one just fifteen, and that old woman – it hardly looks possible. But don't look so shocked, you won't take any notice after an hour or so.

[. . .]

The sun is out warm and strong and there are more signs of life in the camp. This old man of thirty years approaching is like the ones you have seen in the paper, it is as much as he can do to stagger along; the wonder is that he can walk at all. But walk he must – walk, walk, walk until he drops exhausted. See, there is one of those little exhausted bodies now so still, so frail that it looks like death itself. You will see other little huddled heaps as the day wears on.

We are near the big hospital. Does it puzzle you to see that the greater part of the hospital is closed off with a mesh wire fence? Read the notice. 'Typhus'. [. . .] We have to go in here on business. It is like some vast nightmare created by Disney to see these death-like, fleshless bodies all around, isn't it? Yet see them you must. They are there wherever you look. Are you turning over in your mind the thoughts of the suffering and torture that must have brought them so slowly and painfully to this condition? Yes, the words bestial, inhuman and fiendish are too good to describe those responsible for this.

Away from the isolated area, we see more and more of these frail creatures – it is hard to think of them as human beings. There are times when one longs for the sight of blood to add a touch of reality to this uncanny scene; something to prove it really is human beings that we see all around us. Thank God we have no need to go into the wards to see the worst cases – I would rather spend a day in a mortuary than five minutes in there!

C. J. Charters, *37 Kinema Section RAOC, BLA,*
from letter dated Friday 18 May 1945[6]

[April] Today (21st) our C.C.S. began to receive some hundreds of these patients – all women. We had cleared a number of houses (a temporary German military barracks) and prepared beds in every available space. [. . .] I helped to carry some of them in. They weighed three to five stone – less than my little brother aged nine. Acting as interpreter – I had to talk to some of them. One Jewish woman aged about 45, as far as I could guess by her conversation (it was otherwise difficult), said, as soon as she was put in bed, 'Please, I want to go to America. How long I have waited for this moment. They shot my husband and two sons in front of me.' Another said 'Must I die? I am only seventeen.' Another spoke to me in English. She was quite insane.

I was giving each a warm drink – it took one woman a full minute to bring her arm out of the blanket to grip the cup. I simply could not look at these human wrecks for more than a few seconds. I found my eyes filling with tears, and had to turn away from my soldier-comrades. These women were not easily distinguishable – the same formula applied to them all, from the neck downwards – just human skeletons. I hope none of them look at a mirror for the next month, at least. To see themselves would certainly treble their grief. Some of them are beyond human aid and will soon die. But they are happy and look forward to living again even though they might know it is only for a short while.

We could not cope with the situation with our hundred men, and we are fortunate in having the help of many doctors, nurses and girls – themselves prisoners in the camp.

Near our field there is a large German Military Hospital from which we have requisitioned stocks of food, linen and blankets. It is almost unbelievable that they should have been feeding so well, and that only a mile away thousands were starving. The hospital personnel claim to have had no knowledge of the situation in the concentration camp. One of the doctors said to me 'If I, even I, a doctor, tried to enter the camp I would have been shot. Similarly if I had even talked about it.'

Yesterday at 6.30am while we were shaving, three German fighters dived out of the low-hanging clouds and sprayed the Field Ambulance's tents, just fifty yards from us, with cannon-fire. We all stood and watched, rather stupefied. The red crosses were on the ground, for all to see – it couldn't be true. Our C.C.S. was untouched. The Field Ambulance's tents were riddled. Luckily only four men were wounded – one very seriously. He has since died. Such is life...

Since yesterday I have been in charge of a house, holding one hundred and fifty patients, in one of the many blocks of houses being used as the hospital.

The following system has been adopted. Every day, roughly 500 sick (all women) from those who it is thought have some chance of recovering, are brought out of the horror camp to us via the delousing centre. Every day the houses are being hurriedly equipped with beds or improvised straw-filled mattresses. I cannot, simply cannot adequately describe these women – most ghastly sights. Nearly all of them have diarrhoea which is making everything dirty and smelly. All cry out in four or five different languages for hundreds of things they want. Lice are crawling over many of them. We literally shower the anti-louse powder over them. Every now and then one of them dies. The houses are staffed by one male or female doctor and eight nurses or helpers – all ex-internees of the horror camp. All have only recently [re]covered from typhus and/or dysentery themselves and are still weak. [...] I work from 8am until 6pm almost without stopping. We are short of so much, mainly staff and labour. However, gradually, things are beginning to look better. This morning I found two corpses and nine more died today. Their bodies are a ghastly sight – skin stretched tightly over bone. Red Cross workers have come to help (and sometimes hinder). I suppose we must be grateful for any kind of help. The task is so gigantic.

This afternoon my friend and I got into No. 1 Camp once more. I shall never go there again. I cannot bear the scene nor the stench. I watched these people – one could almost *see* them dying as they stood or walked. One girl took two minutes to climb one step to the hut door. She staggered back once and managed it, the second time. The one thing I saw that pleased me was the S.S. men being bullied into work. They collect dead and infected clothing – push their carts by hand and throw the mixed loads into enormous mass graves (5,000 bodies each). All the time our armed troops shout at them, kick them, threaten them, never letting them stop for a moment. What horrible types they were – these S.S. – with their Hollywoodian criminal features. They are being shown no quarter – they know what end is in store for them when their work is finished. One of them, pointed out to me, was previously Commandant of a Polish Concentration Camp.

A film unit, making a propaganda film for compulsory German distribution, got the Chief Doctor of the Camp [amongst the prisoners] (a Polish Jewess, Dr. [Ada] Bimko) whom I was accompanying, to speak into the microphone. She gave a concise account to some of the atrocities [at Auschwitz] – the gas chamber, crematorium, the gynaecology experiments on women – the petrol intravenous injections of the notorious Dr. Klein – the starvation. Her speech brought tears to my eyes. [...]

I wonder how many of my patients will have died by tomorrow morning ...

Today, I was moved to another 'house', prepared to receive more patients. It was merely a repetition of the previous days. Dash here and there. Direct the nurses and Hungarians; organise, command, 'scrounge'. I have never worked so hard before. Each house holds roughly 150 patients – the maximum number normally tended at one time by our *whole* C.C.S.

We, the RAMC men, after nine days of this life, are feeling the tremendous physical and mental strain imposed on us by this vital work of ours. There is simply no time to do anything but eat, work and sleep.

[...]

The last three days have been quite maddening. I have been receiving male patients. Of the eight girls sent to nurse, there are but two who know what they have to do. The rest are too ill in any case, and huddle round the fireplace in their respective wards. There are only thirty beds in the whole building. The rest sleep on poorly filled straw mattresses on the floor. Nearly all have diarrhoea. There are as yet only 12 bed-pans for the 150 patients. Consequently, it takes the nurses 90% of their time to give and remove bed-pans and the urinal-and-faeces buckets originally intended to contain food. The internee doctor – weak, post-typhus, is a Czech Jew, who badly needs medical treatment himself. So weak and dispirited, he could only manage to 'visit' fifty patients throughout the morning. He had been instructed to ascertain which of two diets his patients were fitted for. [...] Most of the patients were put on to diet 2 – which comprises soup, potatoes, bread. [...] Poor, disillusioned men. When they first came – they showered thanks and praise on me, as representative of Britain. They felt, 'Everything is all right now. We will receive lots of food, clothing, cigarettes.' After the plateful of hot, thin soup and half a slice of sour, brown German bread, they began to wonder. Unfortunately when the camp was liberated some idiot had made the fatal mistake of distributing lots of food to these starved wretches. In one hut 80 out of 160 had died from overfeeding in one night. Nevertheless, those men began first to murmur, then beg, then complain, then become hysterical and even cry, 'Let us go back to the camp. We were getting food there!! Do you call this food? Give us some clothes – we will make our own way.' How could they be expected to understand that they were being given medical treatment now, of which carefully planned diet was an essential part? The tea meal (tea plus a slice of bread and butter) and supper (6pm) – more thin soup and bread, satisfied them no more than had the midday meal. They began to rave. Unfortunately – these patients had not been sorted (there was no time for that, I presume) – thus quite a number who were relatively fit had been included. In the evening I gladdened 100 hearts by giving out some of my cigarettes.

I left the house at 7.15, having stayed 1¼ hours extra, through serving the 6 o'clock meal. I was afraid to think about the morrow. I knew there were no fires in the rooms for lack of labour to chop wood and maintain the fires. I knew the morrow's food would be no better nor more plentiful.

My fears were realised the next day. I found that one of the two night nurses had slept all night. Dirty, smelly buckets, blankets and bed-pans were littered all over the building. Even parts of the floor were covered with faeces. There had been no electricity throughout the night, no coffee had been forthcoming from the canteen at 6am. None of the patients had been washed. Nothing but chaos had reigned.

[…]

After my lunch, always a hurried affair, I came back to find my only efficient nurse weeping. She couldn't carry on, she said. The men had rioted during my absence – had run about, naked, searching for food. They had entered the doctor's room and stolen some biscuits I had given him. They had even snatched a large, quite meatless bone. The whole place was in an uproar. 'Food, food, food,' was all I heard. Some of the men were quite out of their minds.

[…]

My RAMC comrades saw my anxious face and told me not to 'take it to heart'. There was nothing I could do about it, they said. At tea-time, I asked the chief nurse to dole out the food herself, since I would not be coming back again, thanks to my leave being due on the morrow. She pleaded with me to accompany her. She was afraid that as soon as she made an appearance with the bread, the men would 'tear her to pieces' in their efforts to grab the food. I insisted – saying she *had* to get used to doing it herself until one of our English nursing sisters started working there. I watched her mount the stairs and listened. After a few seconds there broke out a tremendous uproar. I dashed upstairs – entered the room and saw half of the occupants, stark-naked, scuttling back to their beds. Absolute silence greeted my stern countenance. I reprimanded them and told them to be patient – we were doing our best.

[…]

I am going on leave tomorrow, to London, which I have not seen for 11 months. I should be full of spirit, and happy in anticipation – but I am not. I simply feel tired, spiritually weak and depressed...

Things are improving daily however; the first of our patients (we have brought 6,000 out of the Camp in 8 days) are beginning to live again. Colour is returning to their faces. Some are even walking about, helping. I pray that the same progress will be made by the rest of these unfortunate people. I think it will. It is only a matter of time – but God, how nerve-racking is that time.

Private Emmanuel Fisher, *32 Casualty Clearing Station, RAMC, BLA*[7]

A sports field close to the barracks became a cemetery [in the hospital camp]. Long trenches across the field were scooped out by bulldozer. Bodies were to be laid out side by side, the Jews being interred from one end of the trench, the Christians from the other end until the grave was full, and another opened. On the first day of their gruesome task of burying the corpses, a party of the Wehrmacht soldiers broke down completely. Having deposited about two dozen bodies in the grave, a corporal ripped off his Iron Cross and stamped it in the ground. The rest of the company followed suit and tore off their badges and decorations in sheer disgust.

[...]

Funeral services were conducted daily at 11.00am. The respective Chaplains, and Rabbis with attendant singers, would assemble at that hour. The bodies of the dead wrapped in a sheet or blanket were already laid out side by side on a bed of leafy branches in a trench stretching across the cemetery. Although buried in the same trench Jews and non-Jews were separated [...]. At a later stage when the name and nationality of the deceased was known it became possible to register their place of burial.

Reverend Father Edmund Swift, SJ, Roman Catholic Chaplain to
81 British General Hospital[8]

[The numbers dying were] so vast that one couldn't be very individual [...] the lorry would come in, and they would scoop up all the bodies – I suppose it had to be [like this] – you just marked up how many on a board with chalk [...] so the lorries would know how much room they would have.

One morning, when they were coming round collecting up the bodies [...] there was one Polish family that had got a special grave dug for them. They were so anxious that they wouldn't go into a grave with 2,000 people that they had dug [this separate grave] – I don't know how, whether a soldier had helped them. And they were desperate – they were crying [...] so I went with them [...] to the mortuary. And it was huge – something like a warehouse before the war – enormous, a big high shed. And there were hundreds of bodies there. And they had labels tied on their ankles, of who they were. Well, to go round about a thousand bodies ... and I don't know [...] but about the third ankle I looked at was the name of the one they were looking for. And oh, the jubilation. We got another army lorry, and took the body, and we went with these Polish – I suppose a group of about fifteen – all got into the lorry as well. We went to these woods where they had dug a grave. [...] They were very strict in their religion, and they sang and they mourned. But to them, they had to have a private burial – they couldn't bear this one relation to go into a grave with 2,000 other people.

Norrie Alexander, British Red Cross[9]

Block 44 in the smaller women's camp had been selected for the ceremonial burning. Two large posters had been stuck on to either side of the block, one bearing a swastika, the other a gigantic iron cross, symbols of National Socialism and Militarism. A third poster, in the centre, depicted the stormy face of Hitler. A flagstaff and a wooden platform had been erected thirty yards from the hut. By three o'clock most of the British troops in Belsen had assembled, and three hundred former inmates had come down from the Panzer Training School. Three Wasps – Bren carriers equipped with flame-throwers – stood ready.

'In a few minutes,' said Colonel Bird, 'we are going to burn down the last remaining hut in what was once Belsen concentration camp. I cannot help feeling – the same thought has probably occurred to you too – that in the razing to the ground by fire of this pestilence-ridden camp there is a great symbol. It is, I feel, a symbol of the final destruction for all time of the bestial, inhuman creed of Nazi Germany; the creed by which criminals tried to debase the peoples of Europe to serve their own devilish ends. The British flag has never stood for cruelty and bestiality. That is why it has never yet flown over Belsen Camp. It will fly in a few moments. There too is a symbol; the symbol of the completion of the great task of liberation for which the Allied Nations have striven for six long years, the completion of the task begun by the British Liberation Army when it landed on the beaches of Normandy on June 6th, last year, and the completion, in particular, of the grim but inspiring task with which units of the 2nd Army were confronted here a short while ago.'

Derrick Sington[10]

The other day you told me you were going to the film of Belsen 'Horror' Camp. Many people throughout England will see the film. Few will have missed seeing the pictures in the papers. Yet, how many, I wonder, will really believe it true? How many will say 'Propaganda'? How many will think that the poor creatures shown in these pictures have been specially selected? All too many I am afraid. Yet here, as I write this letter within the camp, is the dreadful evidence to show that the accounts are only lacking truth by concealment of terrible facts and sights which decency itself forbids publishing.

With ironic humour I realise that I should possibly have been the first to cry out: 'Propaganda! selected pictures!' if I had seen the pictures in England, but, like St Thomas, the proof has been put before my eyes. Those pictures that have shocked the world are nothing in comparison to that ghost-like army that line the corridors and fill the rooms of Belsen.

They lie in their beds mute and helpless, with fleshless limbs grotesquely protruding from under the blankets. Lifeless eyes glare out of hollow spaces devoid of flesh; their necks are thinner than my wrist. But I cannot describe the fearful sight. Try to picture a skeleton covered with skin alone; try to picture a skeleton like that with the faintest spark of life in it; try to picture thousands like it ravaged with typhus, dysentery and even worse diseases – picture that in your mind and you know, in part, the truths of Belsen.

[…]

The full story of Belsen has yet to be written, but when the day dawns of its publication this most brutal, inhuman and ghastly Hell on earth will be revealed to the whole world.

I have mentioned nothing of what happened in Belsen before its liberation by the Allies, nor of the sights that met our soldiers' gaze when first they entered, for here I tell you only of my own personal experience of the place.

I do not believe in gloating and publishing the sins of another whether that other be a man or a nation, but this is a crime of which the whole world should know; a crime more fiendish, more cold blooded and calculated than the 'Black Hole of Calcutta'.

I wish I could put this letter in the 'Western Independent' that Westcountry folk could have a Westcountryman's testimony form truth of what they have read and seen in papers and on films.

I wish all men connected with this camp would write home to their folks and local papers and substantiate the truth.

But, above all, I wish that every possible German could be conducted around the camp to see with his own eyes what his blind faith and idolatry of the Nazi creed made possible, or what his fear allowed to continue.

Now, rising above the green of tree and woodland, a column of black rolling smoke ascends, to gradually disperse and blend with the clouds; the first block of Belsen's huts has been fired – Germany is being cleansed of one of its blackest spots; but the crime has yet to be cleansed.

Cherio, my darling,

Your own,

Cyril.

C. J. Charters, *letter dated Tuesday 15 May 1945*

NOTES

1. Paul Kemp, 'The British Army and the Liberation of Bergen-Belsen', in Jo Reilly et al., *Belsen in History and Memory* (London: Frank Cass, 1997), p. 147.
2. Imperial War Museum, Department of Documents (hereafter IWM DD), 85/38/1.
3. From a speech given at the Inter-Allied Conference, June 1945; IWM DD and the Wellcome Archive, London.
4. IWM DD, 94/51/1.
5. IWM Sound Archive 11903/2.
6. IWM DD, Con shelf.

7. IWM DD 95/2/1.
8. IWM DD 90/4/1.
9. IWM Sound Archive, 15441/2.
10. *Belsen Uncovered* (London: Duckworth, 1946), p. 149.

Chapter 3
The Experience of the
Volunteer Medical Teams

In the effort to clear Camp 1 prior to the ceremonial burning of the last hut on 21 May 1945, the military was aided by a number of civilian relief teams sent from Britain and elsewhere.

The British Red Cross sent six relief teams, incorporating one Quaker Relief Team, on 21 April. Surprisingly, their arrival on 25 April was not universally welcomed. 'We felt that they would be just a damn nuisance,' explains Colonel Gonin. But these workers, as Gonin acknowledges, proved invaluable in efforts to clear Camp 1 and establishing arrangements for longer-term health care.

As patients were transferred to Camps 2 and 3 and the Hospital, the death rate fell – from 500 per day during the initial liberation to below 100 by early May. The Red Cross Teams worked primarily in the hospital areas, rather than in Camp 1 itself. Indeed, army rules dictated that the women among these aid groups were not even allowed into the main 'horror' camp.

More help arrived on 30 April: a group of 97 medical students from various London hospitals, all male and most in their early twenties. Originally asked by the Red Cross to assist in famine relief work in Holland, at the last minute it was decided to send them to Belsen. Over the month of May they worked under the auspices of the Red Cross and were supervised by Dr Meiklejohn of the United Nations Relief and Rehabilitation Administration.

The medical students were a unique group. They worked in pairs in Camp 1, and their intense one-month stay is unusually well documented in the testimony archives. As they were exempt from conscription, some expressed guilt at not being called up; many of their schoolfriends would have died in battle. No training could have prepared them for what they were to encounter at Belsen. As Dr L. W. Clarke, a former student at Barts Hospital, recalls: 'I don't think any of my knowledge as a medical student, apart from opening the odd abscess, was really of any use [...] If somebody had pneumonia, you couldn't do anything about it, there was no point in diagnosing it.' As civilians, most of the volunteer relief workers would not have been to battle and, as such, the sights at Belsen would have been even more shocking and out of context. This chapter documents their experience and recognizes the important part they played in the continuing relief operation.

*

After we had been there three or four days, time disappeared at Belsen so I am uncertain of the date, we heard at one of our evening conferences that some BRCS and St John's Ambulance teams were coming to help us. I am telling this tale as it happened and not what you would like to hear. There was a moan of disgust and at least two more bottles than usual were drunk that night. You see it was, as we thought, just some more people to show round, more helpless folk who would have to be looked after. They'll want everything there isn't – bedpans, sheets, blankets, nightdresses. They'll write home saying how awful the conditions are here and why isn't more being done about it. No, there was despair and despondency in the ranks that night. We felt that they would be just a damn nuisance.

I was detailed to meet them and to show them where they were to live with the very definite instructions that as they had come they would have to look after themselves. The first one I saw was a lady dressed in the grey uniform of the Society of Friends. She looked pretty fierce to me but I asked if there was anything I could do and had they found their accommodation? 'Yes', she said, 'We're alright, come and have a gin.' I thought to myself, 'Well, you've got the right idea anyway.' I never changed my opinion and I should love to talk for hours about the BRCS and St John's. They were superb, they tackled every job under the sun and what's more they didn't have to be told what to do. No job was too big, no job too dirty, no job too tedious for them to undertake. If one was tired and dispirited and everything seemed to be going wrong one had only to go and see Elsie or Vivian or Tony (I don't think I ever learnt their surnames) and in a very few minutes one felt on top of the world.

The girls were far better than we were in raping the German civilian population for comforts and food for the internees. There was no job they didn't want to tackle. One girl even wanted to relieve my chaps in driving the death cart which collected the bodies of those who died in the Hospital area. There was only one thing which upset them and upset them it did in a big way, and that was when one of the English papers referred to them as the 'Heroines of Belsen'. I really believe that Belsen would still be in a state of chaos if they had not arrived.

*Lieutenant-Colonel **M. W. Gonin**, Commanding Officer,*
11 Light Field Ambulance, RAMC[1]

THEIR NAMES 'MUST NOT BE REVEALED' –
BRITISH HEROINES OF BELSEN

A group of British women, sisters of Q.A.I.M.N.S. and members of the British Red Cross Society, played what was described by the senior R.A.M.C. medical officer as an 'absolutely superb' part in the gigantic relief task at Belsen concentration camp, writes a military observer.

Though not asked to work among the horrors of the concentration camp itself, these women had to bear conditions almost equally harrowing and appalling.

For several weeks without respite they handled daily hundreds of starved, desperately weak people whom disease and persecution had turned into sub-humans.

In nightmare conditions, with typhus prevalent, these British women strove, often for 14 to 16 hours a day, to save the lives of their thousands of patients.

Rules demand that the British women of Belsen, whose fortitude saved thousands of lives, remain anonymous.

From the Evening Standard *– 5 June 1945*

The arrival of 97 medical students from the London Training Hospital[s] proved the greatest help and with their advent the death rate, which in the earliest days had been 500 per day, began to drop appreciably. With their knowledge and enthusiasm we were able to exercise much better supervision in each hut; they worked splendidly and I cannot speak highly enough of their efforts under the guidance of Dr Meiklejohn.

Brigadier H. L. Glyn-Hughes, RAMC, DDMS 2nd Army, BLA[2]

We thought, 'oh, what a bloody nuisance they're [the London medical students] going to be', but they were far from it – they were fantastic [. . .] We were so – not full of our own self-importance – but we were so busy ourselves in looking after mundane things that we thought 'what the hell are they going to be doing?' But in actual fact they helped with the very, very sick and they actually fed an awful lot of the people who couldn't feed themselves.

Major Alexander Smith Allan, *113 Light Anti-Aircraft Regiment*[3]

Belsen Concentration Camp, 5 May 1945
Dear Mr Groves,

Maybe you will be surprised when you open this letter and find that it is from me in Germany, but I'll explain the whole situation I hope satisfactorily. Wasn't it great news today that all the German Armies opposing 21st Army Group had surrendered[?] We celebrated in the SS Panzer Grenadier Officers Mess in Belsen Camp with some 'liberated' wine! Afterwards feelings were liberated and an incredible Polish brass band arrived suddenly outside and began to blow away furiously. They played, many didn't find the right notes of one tune till the next, but they played to our cheers and applause first of all some Central (?) European marches and then God Save the King, majestically this, and the Polish National Anthem and then of all things 'Roll out the Barrel'! They were tickled to death when we burst forth into song so played it through three times and went away with much clicking of heels and hand waves. It makes one really feel that this job of cleaning out probably largest human cess pit in the world is really providing results when one sees the unlimited expressions of illimitable gratitude shown here.

To explain how or why we came here may I start a month ago? The British Red Cross were at this time appealed to by 21st Army Group to supply medical attention and correct diet for the thousands of Dutch people who were starving on account of the railway strike. They estimated that they would not be remotely able to cope with the situation by themselves. So the British Red Cross in turn appealed for 100 students in their final 18 months from the London Medical Schools to do this work. Twelve volunteers were asked for from St. Thomas's and I was lucky enough to be one of the chosen. The whole scheme however was altered when Holland was liberated so slowly and we waited and waited until suddenly at 3hrs notice we were told to prepare to be off to Belsen! We had previously been equipped with ordinary army battle dress etc., and started having our inoculations. So we were off with our predigested protein and glucose vitamin preparations. You have probably read quite a deal about the whole scheme in the papers. The Sunday Graphic said we landed in Germany last Sunday morning whereas in reality our Dakota could not take off till Tuesday owing to weather conditions.

Well we arrived and came to our superb billets that same night. I say superb because we are living in the SS Panzer Grenadier Training Barracks, a super modern Sandhurst with electric light and running water in each room, even table lamps beside the beds.

To get on to Belsen Camp: we go there everyday of the week and work from 8am till 6pm, with 1¼ hrs break for lunch. I feel dead at the end of it. That is not the end though for we have a conference from 6.15–7.15 to check upon the chaos here. There is then a council from about 9.30 onwards from Group Leaders and various officials that have been appointed. We are run by two doctors one in UNRRA [Meiklejohn] and the other in the RAMC [Gonin] a veritable firebrand who has worked miracles. He is a Czech and speaks 7 languages.

[. . .]

The position as regards we medical students is this. Each one is in charge of a hut and it is his job to see that the inmates are properly fed. For this job we brought over big supplies of glucose vitamin mixture and predigested milk protein. I have a women's hut in which there were 160 people badly ill. Almost all have starvation diarrhoea and are lying huddled almost on top of each other wallowing in filth and crying for attention. On average four die every day and their bodies are removed and buried by the Wehrmacht. Death and evacuation to two hospitals which have been set up have now reduced the number to 115. The stench of these filthy emaciated bodies has long ceased to bother me, and they have long ceased to have any sense of feminine decency or modesty.

Each hut is run by a man or woman called the Block fuehrer whose job it is to instil some form of order and keep a tally of the inmates. He or she is usually quite well fed and in moderately good health. Many of them used to work and so had extra rations. They are usually quite young. My block fuehrer is a Greek girl of twenty-one who speaks excellent French; and thank goodness for that otherwise the chaos would have been far greater since 95% of the hut are Polish! I am however fast getting a command of necessary German, and now and again can raise an odd word in Russian, Czech, Polish or Hungarian.

Well, having worked from 8am till 6pm for five days [it] seems as if this chaos of life and death in rotting buildings may soon produce some sign of order. The RAMC and the RA regiment who liberated Belsen have worked miracles. The latter are doing all the catering for these thousands of people and I consider that to suddenly change one's occupation from that of firing a field gun to running six huge kitchens is a feat to be proud of.

Of course there is no science of medicine attached to the job at the moment. Scientific treatment in a human cesspit is impossible but it will nevertheless come in time: indeed it has already come in our two hospital blocks. It is however extraordinarily interesting from the physiological point of view to watch the reactions of starving people to different kinds of food, and to observe the incidence of famine oedema. I should have mentioned though that the whole thing is complicated by the fact that most of the starved have either typhus or T.B. as well.

I hope that this account of Belsen has interested you. I make no apologies for any detail in fact I could have elaborated ad infinitum: but that would probably not improve a picture which to start with is really indescribable. I would never have believed had I not seen this. Of this I have no doubt that all that has passed in Belsen, Buchenwald and Dachau etc. should be shouted round the world as the greatest anti-German propaganda ever.

And now I must stop albeit too soon and it remains only for me to send my regards to Mrs Groves, Pat, Biddy and Sister and to all of Johnson's.
Yours sincerely,
Michael H. Coigley
     Dr Michael Coigley, *former medical student at St Thomas's Hospital*[5]

[S]everal of us volunteered to go to feed the starving Dutch, and then we suddenly got the call one day to report to Lowndes Square the next day, where a lady with a greet deal of silver braid said that we would be better occupied in Belsen in the concentration camp which had just been liberated. But she said that anybody who didn't wish to go could pull out there and then, but nobody did. [...] I think in some respects we were pleased that we were going to do something that we might think was of some use in the War since we had so many friends who'd gone away and we would never see again. And we felt a bit out of it really, since we were in a reserved occupation.

[. . .]

We settled in one day, and I think we had a sort of conference that night in the big mess hall. The next day we were taken down to the concentration camp itself. I think the first day we were taken down. I think after that we had to hitch lifts, and it was about two miles away, that I remember very well because it seemed that the chaps who you hitched the lifts from used to delight in bumping you along this road as fast as possible. [. . .] Another thing that sticks out in my memory, is that we used to have to go through a hut where we were covered in DDT literally, hats off, blow it in your hair, up your sleeves and down your trousers. And every day we had this when we went in because I think mainly they were worried we would get lice which were prevalent, and it was believed that the typhus was mainly spread via the lice. This was not thought to be true later on, it was thought to be dust-borne. But anyway, it was as well not to get any lice and the DDT I think did this. What else it did I don't know.

[. . .]

I don't think they told us much about what to expect. I think it had been in the papers in England and I think they said it's much as you've been told in the papers [. . .] They were obviously authentic photographs that had been taken [. . .] I think my first impression was that it confirmed my preconceived ideas that the press had actually been very factual on this. This dusty vast array of wooden huts separated down the middle by a sort of dirt track, barbed wire keeping people where they thought they should be. And then this vast array of people shuffling. Nobody seemed to lift their feet. Nobody seemed to have the strength to lift their feet. And from time to time you came across people who were obviously dead. All of the people seemed to be emaciated. The smell still lingers on in the memory, difficult to describe, but I'm sure if I ever smelt it again it would come back to me. [. . .] The smell of decay, smoke as well, because they had started to burn some of the mess in the camp, because I think it was still ten days to a fortnight after it was liberated. So they had actually been burying the bodies that had died. I think when we arrived they'd buried the bodies up to three days before, a backlog of about three days.

1 The memorial to the Jews murdered in Bergen-Belsen. The stone is set on the site of one of the mass graves in the notorious Camp No. 1.

2 British army personnel in protective clothing entering one of the huts at Bergen-Belsen concentration camp.

3 British soldiers searching SS men for arms.

4 The burial pit dug by bulldozer. In the background are the tents in which some prisoners lived before the British army took over.

5 British army medics taking care of a typhus patient at Bergen-Belsen concentration camp.

6 British soldiers and women inmates queuing at Belsen camp.

7 A damaged military ambulance and British soldiers in protective clothing at Belsen camp.

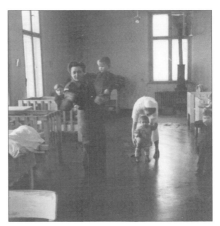

8 The children's TB ward in Glyn Hughes Hospital, Bergen-Belsen Displaced Persons' Camp.

9 People collecting logs outside the living quarters in Bergen-Belsen Displaced Persons' Camp. The barracks formerly housed SS Panzer units.

10 Queuing for milk in Bergen-Belsen Displaced Persons' Camp.

11 A young woman preparing a meal in Bergen-Belsen Displaced Persons' Camp

12 Hanging out washing, winter, Bergen-Belsen Displaced Persons' Camp.

13 Administrative staff meeting at Glyn Hughes Hospital, Bergen-Belsen Displaced Persons' Camp.

14 A Jewish TB patient doing handicraft work. An occupational therapist from the Jewish Relief Unit provides instructions and materials.

15 The handing-over ceremony of a police car to the Jewish police.

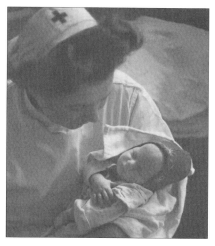

16 A woman prepares a meal from the meagre rations at Camp 2, Bergen-Belsen.

17 One of the many babies born in Belsen hospital.

18 Life at the nursery, Bergen-Belsen Displaced Persons' Camp. The nursery was under the supervision of the Jewish Relief Unit's Children's Welfare Officer, Miss Hindle Pearlman.

19 Former inmates of Belsen concentration camp fetching water laid on by the British military.

20 Former women prisoners of Belsen concentration camp having a meal.

21 An expert shoe-maker working in the corner of his room in Bergen-Belsen Displaced Persons' Camp.

22 The first train for Palestine draws out from the very siding at Belsen to which many people were brought by the Nazis.

[...]

At first I was paired with a chap called Ian Jackson, and subsequently a man I shared a room with, which was David Bradford. [...] Hut 240 was very much better than the majority of the huts there. It did contain some children, and apparently they had tried to guide the children in the concentration camp to Hut 240, and had also tried to get into that hut any nurses that they discovered. So they did manage to make this reasonable, if that's the word – it was much better than the other huts.

I suppose there were about three hundred in this hut, whereas in a similar sized hut of one of my colleagues there'd be somewhere like six hundred [...] most of them were utterly emaciated. Some had died, some were about to die. In this particular hut there were one or two who were reasonably fit, and I gathered from them that they were reasonably fit because they'd only been in the place about a month, so they hadn't had time to starve. There didn't seem to be a lot of actual disease in that actual hut, again probably because they had some people there who did know something about nursing, but how much this helped in those circumstances I don't know. One of the problems of course was the language situation, and I asked if anybody could speak English, and many people said 'Yes, yes' but then you found the only thing that they could say was yes or no.

[...]

In fact that hut was so much better than the other huts that I went back to the lady who allocated us our huts and said 'Look, there's not a lot we can do in that hut, they're so well organised compared with the others, would you please give me another job?' which she did. [... S]he put me in charge of the field radios the first day because somebody had to man the field radio because this was the only means of communication with the outside world. And I did that for two or three days, and I think on the second or third day I heard Churchill come across saying that the War was over in Europe and I was actually on the field radio when this came through. And I managed then to get somebody else to keep the field radio while I went round to tell the inmates. I got a friend of mine to go round the men's side while I went round the women's side, thinking of course they'd be, well not exactly over the moon but at least relieved. They were so apathetic. [...] [With o]ne or two it raised a cheer, not many, they were too far gone.

[...]

[T]hey were trying to evacuate the people, clean them up, put them through what we called a human laundry, put them into decent surroundings. And they were taking them down the road so that eventually they went though this so-called human laundry, and they were scrubbed by German nurses. Then they had completely clean clothes on. They went into clean beds. The main one was in Huhne [Höhne] itself.

But that didn't go through fast enough so they asked me to organise one in the camp itself. And they managed to clean up one hut and get straw palliasses into this. They managed to find some showers, and so at least they could put some people temporarily into better accommodation. And I remember vividly doing that for a few days because I remember many of them very weak, and I had to help them through the showers. And then they were sprayed with DDT again, into their palliasses.

And I can remember one very frail chap. And I discovered he was an ex-professor. And when I got him tucked up in bed and safe and put a blanket over him he grabbed me by the arm and would not let me go. He kissed my arm all the way up and all the way down, and he nearly had a fit saying 'Hitler, Hitler – I kill Hitler!'

And also I remember while I was doing this particular job a unit of RAF chaps who'd been delegated to go round and find war criminals, or people they suspected of being war criminals [arrived]. And one of these chaps came in while I was helping in this human laundry, and he asked me about it, and then he said, 'I've been given this job of finding war criminals. I wasn't really keen on the job at all, I didn't really have much incentive – by golly I've got an incentive now.' And he went off seeing that he could do something on that line.

[. . .]

There was a problem with the food because if you gave them a proper diet then their stomachs couldn't take it because they'd been without good food for a long time. They had a bio-chemist there who was producing some tasteless stuff which I don't think seemed to do an awful lot of good, some hydrolisate I think. But by and large there were stews, things of that nature. People were mainly starving because the system of keeping order in the concentration camp had been that they had one bit at the end of the hut separated off from the rest. And in this bit they had what was called a blockleader who in many cases had been a German criminal.

And the food was always delivered to the blockleader who took out what she or he [. . .] wanted and gave it to a few favourite friends and then what was left over was distributed to the people at the other end of the hut. But most of them hadn't had any nourishment at all for a long time.

But indeed, after a few days I think we universally hit upon the idea that we should make one person who was ambulant responsible for a person who couldn't get up, and take him the food. In other words they couldn't have their own food unless they took one to somebody else. And I think we all managed to do this and saved probably a few lives that way.

[. . .]

I happened to pal up with a couple of chaps who had been sent, I think, from the RASC, to sort out the huge collection of watches which had been found at the camp. I gather that when the Germans had the truce with the British, that there would be a take over, that three cartloads were despatched from the concentration camp. The first cartload contained, apparently, wines, the second cartload was alleged to contain jewellery and rings, and the third cartload contained watches. Apparently a few people saw these go. They told the British about the watches whereupon the British promptly found these watches and dug them up, and they occupied quite a fair sized room which I saw, which was knee-deep in watches. Apparently the people in the know, when they saw the British did this, they didn't tell them where the wine was, they didn't tell them where the jewellery was. But apparently some of the inmates used to go out at night and come back with arms full of bottles of wine. [. . .]

The method of selecting what happened to the watches was that these chaps had instructions to pick up a watch, wind it twice, shake it twice, and if it went, it went on one side and went back to the army, and if it didn't tick it was chucked away. And there were some lovely watches there, gold Omegas, vast numbers. [. . .] I think [such items were] so far removed from [the former inmates that] I don't think they realised there was any chance [of retrieving such goods]. They presumably had accumulated over the years, [and belonged] not just [to] the recent ones in there. I don't know how many watches there were, but there must have been an accumulation of several months any way, if not years, for the numbers. No, I think the people there, the ones that survived, were just glad to have survived, weren't thinking of anything going back to them at all.

[. . .]

The nearest you could see to a crematorium was a large ex-oven in which there were three stretchers on racks, is probably the better way of putting it, and nearby this, the fuel which was used for this were the dried shoes of the people who'd been to the camp. And outside the door was this mountain of shoes as big as a normal house. It was pretty definite these had been used as a fuel.

[. . .]

[The inmates] seemed strangely reluctant to tell you [about their internment] because it was so appalling they just said 'Ah, what's the use of reiterating it'. But there was just one time when my interpreter broke down and she then told me. And that was the day that they were going to burn that hut, our hut. And I went past, and they'd got all of the people out of it, and we went to see that nothing was left. And she suddenly started to burst into tears, and I asked her why she was bursting into tears now when it was more or less a happy time that the hut was going to be burnt. And she then told me that six months before it was snowing, that it was thought unfit for the girls to take them down to the place where they worked which was apparently down the road.

And she said that instead they got them out at six in the morning as usual and made them stand outside their hut with their hands on their head until six o'clock at night, in the snow. And if they fell down they beat them until they stood up again or died. That was the only time that I really heard any direct evidence of physical maltreatment or torture, whatever you like to call it. But I think simply because they didn't want to tell you, didn't want to know any more.

[...]

One of my friends – I remember very well indeed meeting him between his hut and mine, where there was a woman sitting on the ground howling away. And she had no mouth or most of her mouth – the lips, had disappeared, a condition which you call *cancrum oris* which is associated with longstanding starvation. And she was moaning and obviously in a lot of pain. And this pal of mine said 'Have you got a morphia handy?' and I said 'I'll go back to the hut and get some'. And I went back to the hut to get some and we met again – and when we came back we couldn't find her. We never found her again, which was not difficult because there were so many people shuffling aimlessly around. It was often quite difficult to find a person again. [...] She just shuffled off into the crowd. She didn't know that we were going to go and get something for her. My chum was going to take her into a hut I think and give her the injection, give her a bit of 'special' supervision. This one tended to do. You could see that people were, perhaps if you did put a bit time in, see they did get fed, then it was just possible that that particular one might be saved. Others you knew they weren't going to be saved, you could see they were dying.

And one particular instance of this was one lady who had two daughters by her. I thought one of her daughters was her mother, and apparently they were twins of eighteen, and they looked like twins of sixty or seventy. I didn't really think there was a hope, but she pleaded with me, and pleaded with me, 'Please can you do something?' So I did get them some priority in getting them moved to where they could get the food which they hoped would be of some use. Unfortunately it didn't seem to work any better then the rest, and I gather they died the next day. No, we didn't really use any medicine [...] it was so difficult supervising them even getting food, I don't know how we could possibly have supervised them getting any actual medicine really. But I think this was taken care of once they'd gone through the human laundry. Everything was so haphazard until then, 'til the place [Camp 1] was actually burnt.

[...]

As far as I'm concerned there wasn't any sanitation at all. The excrement was just between the floorboards that were missing. In all the huts that I went in there were some floor-boards that just weren't there, and these were conveniently used by the inmates as a sort of latrine, if you like to call it that. But then outside the huts they just squatted where they could, so it was just as bad really, less concentrated, but just as bad outside the huts.

But the people that I think did even more than we did for their benefit were the Quakers who [. . .] got fresh water to Belsen. And they seemed to have no fear, they didn't mind what they did, and they worked very hard, and I had a great respect for them. And of course water was probably more important than the food, and that did provide some minor sanitation later. They could go to the end of a hosepipe and at least get some water from that to wash with. But otherwise I didn't see any sanitation in my hut at all.

[. . .]

I don't think any of my knowledge as a medical student, apart from opening the odd abscess, was really of any use; I can't think where. If somebody had pneumonia, you couldn't do anything about it, there was no point in diagnosing it. So I don't know – where would the medicine have come in, knowledge of medicine? Common sense, and as most of us then were, reasonably fit, youth, able to carry on and do things [. . .] we felt that at least now we could do something for the war effort, relief. Anything that one could do made it seem worthwhile that there'd been a battle really. I always had doubts as a boy and ever since as to what ever was achieved by the First World War. It seemed to me that if we'd lost the First World War I don't know, but I don't see that things would have been all that much worse then when we won it. But I'd no doubts about the second one. If ever there was a war worth fighting I think Belsen confirms it.

[. . .]

I don't remember feeling frightened [. . .] mind you we didn't come up against any bullets, and I think we were used to going round wards with diseased people. So we had seen people who were dying of cancer who looked just as emaciated as these people. I suppose to some extent we'd met the awful things of life. It was just the enormity of it, you didn't just meet one. But I think because we were all there together as well, all of much the same age, and the evenings I think one got rebound. You didn't sit down and brood. You sat down, all chaps together and made the best of what was a bad job, but I think you got some rebound, and you almost laughed more in the evenings than one normally would.

Dr L. W. Clarke, *former medical student at Barts Hosptial*[5]

[B]eing medical students, we felt perhaps that we were rather feather bedded. Our friends were all in the army, the navy and so on, and had had quite a hectic time. I'd lost several friends who had been at school with me, in the navy and the air force. And this was our chance to get away and to do something, perhaps slightly different, to help the War effort.

[...]

We wore battledress with a Red Cross flash. And this made it rather confusing for other military personnel because they didn't quite know what we were. They weren't sure whether we were officers or whether we were other ranks. One moment we were civilians and the next moment we were strutting about in battledress.

[...]

My inmates were nearly all male. The camp was divided into a women's section and a [male] section. But as time went by we called these three huts that had been done up a sort of very primitive hospital. And we managed to [...] tidy it up a bit and get it a bit cleaner. And also there were some doctors there. There was a Russian doctor and Czech doctors who had been inmates, who tried to help us try to get some sort of order into it, and to start treating the patients and so on.

[...]

Well then gradually the hut became empty and we were told that as the time went by the sicker ones were going to be moved up into Bergen where there was a military hospital, a German military hospital. One wing of this hospital was used for British personnel, one ward I suppose really. And the rest of it was to be used for people who had been moved from Belsen camp into better accommodation where there were actually beds. I can't remember whether there were sheets and things. I think there were paper sheets and paper towels which the Germans had left behind. And this was staffed by German nurses who had been left behind. I suppose they had been originally working in the military hospital. They hadn't retreated with the German troops because they'd been left there. There were very good X-ray facilities there. And as time went by, as Belsen was emptied, we were each given fifty or sixty patients in the new hospital at Bergen.

And we could begin to examine them and just see what we had got. One part was kept separate for typhus cases, obviously. There was a lot of tuberculosis. We could get their chest X-rayed, and it was quite an efficient service. You'd fill in a form and they would be taken down to the X-ray department by orderlies. And then the next day you'd get an X-ray report. And of course in those days with tuberculosis there was no chemotherapy like there is now when the treatment was simply nourishment, bedrest and fresh air really. There wasn't anything else you could do. Other things we had to treat – we had to treat a lot of abscesses, bedsores, and of course their general condition was poor. People who had poor nourishment, they are likely to get secondary infections and urinary infections and pneumonia and this sort of thing. And we were able to treat these things once we'd got the patients, and once we were able to examine them and make some form of diagnosis, we were able to treat them with this sulphonamide that was [...] available in those days.

And we could then begin to see a little bit of daylight probably. There was a time scale – the first fortnight really we were cleaning out Belsen itself. That was the part when we were actually in the huts. And the first week we didn't have any time off at all. We worked eleven days flat out. And after that we were given a morning off a week and an afternoon off on another day. And it was insisted that we should do this because it was fairly hard work, and also it was a bit of an ordeal because we were pretty young. I think that being young as we were – I was about twenty three years old I suppose at that time – one could stand it more. I think that if one had been more mature – I think if one had to face it now and realise that these people who were in this terrible state were human beings and were somebody's mothers and fathers, and sons and so on and so forth, I don't think one could have borne it. But as it was, they were almost as unrecognisable as human beings. And of course we were young medical students.

These people were all foreign, they couldn't speak English. We had an interpreter. I had a young Pole who had been a medical student in Cracow. And he was able to speak a bit of English, and he used to help us in our hut to try and get some sort of communication going. But as I say, people say to me, how could you possibly stand it? But it was I think that we were young and much more flexible, and could take it in those days.

[. . .]

Since I've been in general practice people say 'Why don't you get 'flu and why don't you get various things?' One just doesn't think [. . .] of that sort of thing, you just go and do it. After all, people who work in fever hospitals and so on, you have vaccinations and so on, but you don't think of that. Some of us were afflicted with diahorrea. I had one day off with diahorrea, but otherwise I didn't think of it at all.

But one of our members – there were two actually, two Barts men, one definitely had typhus and had to be flown home, and another one was suspected, but I don't think he actually had it. I think he just had a nasty tummy upset or something like that. But we didn't think of that at all really. One or two of us got the odd boil which I suppose was quite likely because if you had a crack in the skin and you're carting these people about, it was very likely that an infection would get in, and you'd get a boil or an abscess like that.

[. . .]

I think a nurse could have done [our job] just as well. We were half trained doctors. Also one was used to a certain amount of illness and unpleasantness, but I think that perhaps it was obviously useful having medical knowledge, but I wouldn't pretend that we were indispensable as doctors. I think that it could have been done by orderlies probably just as well. All that you had to do was supervise that the food went round really in the first part, and that those who couldn't help themselves were helped. Latterly in the other hospital the medical knowledge did come in helpful, because we were able to examine the people and wash them, clean them, and so on and so forth, and we were able to try to make some sort of diagnosis.

Dr D. C. Bradford, former medical student at Barts Hosptial[6]

[The Red Cross] wasn't like the army, it was a little bit more friendly, and not so disciplined. When we got to Belsen there was no discipline at all really – you just had to do what came along – there were no set rules or anything [. . .] you didn't report to Sister everything you did – you just had to get on with it. [. . .] We were rather left to our own devices, because it was almost too much to try and organise. I suppose everyone just helped where they could. The food was delivered to each barracks [. . .] and we would take it to them, and perhaps to the very ill ones, we might try to help get a little fluid into them. So it was – I don't think crude nursing – but just trying to keep them alive.

Norrie Alexander, British Red Cross[7]

For the first few days we had great difficulties in serving meals. Armed guards were placed on duty as patients who could stand threw themselves on the food vessels, snatched at platefuls of food and fought like savages for a slice of bread.

Some of the most feeble of these starving persons had first to be nourished with liquid food, followed by diet meals but it was difficult to make them understand why they could not eat as much as they pleased.

Life in our hospital-centre was quite different from anything we have ever experienced. It seemed to us sometimes that we were living on another planet; we had in fact to forget all our habits, our ideas as to tidiness, cleanliness, moral considerations and human dignity in order to try and comprehend our patients' psychological and mental state.

We no longer had rules to guide us and it was quite impossible for us to imagine the depths of suffering endured by these unfortunate people over the past years.

The question of languages raised yet another difficulty. In addition to numerous dialects, 22 official languages were spoken in the camp. I can hardly believe now that we managed to understand the stories told by our patients in a foreign language. When they spoke in their mother tongue, and in their dialect in particular, their speech was more spontaneous and we understood them better than if it were partially interpreted.

When they tried to describe their harrowing experiences the past came back so vividly that we were able, from their gestures and the expression on their faces, to understand what they were trying to tell us.

When we ourselves tried to express ourselves in the same manner we found that we had to learn to co-ordinate gestures and words with our thoughts.

Luckily we found among the internees some who had knowledge of western languages as well as Slav and Baltic dialects. Their services were the most useful, especially for the registration of the patients; they were later allowed to work in the camp interpreter's office.

Anny Pfirter, *British Red Cross*[8]

We had to move our quarters on Saturday which was a great bore; packing up to move one mile is as bad as packing to move across Europe, as we have now collected a certain amount of furniture as well as all our equipment. I am not working quite so hard recently, my three kitchens seem to be organised at last in spite of my B.R.C. assistant being taken away with scarlet fever. I was just beginning to enjoy a bit of leisure, but alas no peace for the wicked, tomorrow I have to report at the evacuation camp and organise feeding for 7,000 refugees in quarantine preparatory to being sent home. I feel quite petrified of the mob and hope there is plenty of British protection at the camp. At the moment I have no idea even of the location.

Our new quarters are in the village in a semi-detached modern house with seven rooms. We are now fourteen so are not too crowded. I share a room with a large covered loggia with Joan, so we do very well. We have a large garden with plenty of soft fruit which will be very welcome in a few weeks if we can prevent the Russians from pinching it. Sister and I visited the local burgomaster and demanded two maids who are proving most excellent and do everything including the household wash, and our room have [*sic*] fresh flowers every day. So much for fraternization. They also tell us that they will prevent the Russians from pinching our things. Altogether this is such an amazing place that I have forgotten who are allies and who are enemies. The Russians are the terror of the countryside and the sooner they are sent home the better for everybody!

19th [May] I am sorry I was not able to finish my letter but I was sent to a new job which has definitely been occupying all my time. I am now messing officer of Camp 3 which is a much bigger job than I anticipated, as it is feeding 1,200 people for three meals a day. I now work for the military government and not the R.A.M.C. I have six sergeants and 18 corporals to keep order in the kitchens and dining rooms, and 120 cooks and kitchen hands of all nationalities, and six interpreters. The military are AA gunners who have been shooting aircraft all the war and now that they are not required are policing these camps. They are marvellous men and have made an excellent job of this camp. They are very nice with the people, although they have to fire a few rounds now and then to keep order between Russians and Poles, and also to prevent looting which of course is rife. I was very sorry to leave the hospital where I had made so many friends, but I think this will be most interesting when I get the run of it. We have quite an amusing mess at the

Military Government Office where all the authorities seem to assemble and it is quite interesting talking to all these different people. I had to apply for an assistant and fortunately Ursula was sent, so altogether things seem to work out well. There are at present only four B.R.C. people at the camp, the others are Welfare Officers. Yesterday there were tremendous thrills when 300 French, Dutch, and Belgian D.P.'s left for home. That was the first evacuation and from now on we are sending hundreds home every day. The trouble is that a great many people especially the Poles have no wish to return home as they are so terrified of the Russians, so I do not know what will happen to them. The whole thing must be a great problem. Every day I have girls crying round me saying they can't go home and will I arrange for them to go to England. I must say I hope the British won't be so kind hearted as to invite them all! Although the individual cases are very pathetic.

Miss Margaret Wyndham Ward, *British Red Cross Society,*
letter of 15 May 1945[9]

REPORT ON CLOTHING IN HOSPITAL SECTION, BELSEN CAMP

Clothing became an urgent problem a few days after the hospital was opened. It was needed first for the 'internee' staff who in most cases had nothing but the clothes in which they stood up, and also for the convalescent patients who had nothing at all, and who were beginning to wander round the stone corridors and out into the open, barefoot and clad only in blankets and pyjamas. Jane Leverson and one of the Red Cross Welfare Officers were asked to organise the distribution of clothing to the "internee" staff and patients respectively. About 8,000 people were to be clothed in the hospital alone.

Supplies were obtained by the Army and to a smaller extent by the Red Cross. Some, new things, came from England and America, but large quantities of second-hand clothes and shoes were commandeered by the Army from civilians in the surrounding districts of Germany – we are told that people had to give up 20% of their wardrobe. The clothes thus obtained varied greatly in quantity and required a great deal of sorting, which is being done by 'internee' workers under the supervision of Red Cross workers. Unfortunately, the Army apparently never thought of compelling the civilians to tie their shoes together and the result is an enormous pile of odd shoes of the most depressing variety. Those of us who worked at Witley have been amused to meet the same voluminous Early Victorian drawers which we sent to Greece. The Russian peasants appreciate them – in fact one can usually tell a Russian by the sort of knickers she chooses – otherwise these garments are useful as 'comic turns' and as material for handkerchiefs. Incidentally, bales of assorted garments and sizes are very tiresome at this end – bales of one type only are much easier to distribute.

DISTRIBUTION

a) to 'internee' staff: Jane Leverson, Elizabeth Clarkson and the Welfare officer from another Red Cross team undertook the distribution to 'internee' doctors, nurses and kitchen staff. This had to be done chiefly in one small room and part of a hospital corridor. Just under 500 people were clothed here. Customers were given personal attention and a record similar to a card index system was kept of clothes given. This was particularly valuable in securing equitable distribution, as at first supplies were erratic and it was not always possible to give everyone her full allowance of 1 dress or skirt, 1 blouse, 2 pairs knickers, 2 pairs stockings, 2 vests, petticoat, coat and a pair of shoes, at one visit. In addition to this the hospital store once produced clothing for 300 people at 4 hours notice.

b) distribution to patients: Since the original premises were too cramped, the retail centre, known as 'Harrods' was moved to a large stable where it was organised on the cafeteria principle. 250–300 patients a day, who have been passed as fit by a doctor, are brought by ambulance, 15 at a time, to get their clothes. The largest section is the women's, as the majority of patients are female, but there is a smaller Men's section upstairs. The main sorting and storing centre remains outside the hospital area.

CONTROL OF DISTRIBUTION

A detailed list of clothes supplied to each individual is no longer kept, now that larger numbers of people are being dealt with, partly owing to shortage of time and partly because it is assumed that now that larger supplies are available, the client can obtain everything in one visit, so that a record of her name is sufficient. It has been found most important to check each customer's goods on departure, both from the practical necessity of stretching supplies and also because it is good for morale. Undoubtedly, some people have got away with more than their fair share, partly because our own checking has not been infallible and also because both Harrods and the store room have been broken into on more than one occasion – they now have to have armed guards. Some of the looters were caught and some of the loot retrieved, but by no means all. Pilfering is a very interesting problem in this camp, but is outside the scope of this report. Another interesting point is, that as one might expect, some of our customers, though practically naked, are extremely fussy. Though this is trying when one is very busy we feel it is a sign of returning self-respect, for many of these people would once have been most particular about their personal appearance. Other factors come into it, but though it is fascinating to explore there, it must not be done in this report.

Harrods Staff fluctuates, but consists of about 6 BRCS workers, 4 internee workers, and 3 or 4 Hungarian orderlies. As soon as more 'internee' staff can be obtained, it should be possible to release some British workers for other jobs. Jane Leverson and Elizabeth Clarkson have both left to act as Welfare Officers in Camps 1 and 4 respectively. The situation is complicated by the fact that physically fit internees are evacuated as soon as possible now, so that not only is it essential to clothe them speedily, but one's Staff may literally be here today and gone tomorrow. Checking and final responsibility for organisation and policy must remain in the hands of the British staff.

CONCLUSION

As a rough estimate, 1,800 people have been clothed to date, and on the whole the organisation has worked well. There is very great danger of a bottle neck, if clothes are given out from Harrod's and the other distribution centres in Camps 3 and 4 more quickly than they can be commandeered and sorted. I am not absolutely certain, but understand that the surrounding country is now our main supply source; much better than nothing, but not absolutely satisfactory. Speed is of considerable importance, since it is hoped that the majority of internees will have left Belsen in a fortnight's time.

Elizabeth J. Clarkson, 18.5.45

Beth Clarkson, *Friends' Relief Service*[10]

When we first came to Belsen I was attached to the children's hospital [...] At that time the children were all in one building, the sick at one end and the 'well' children at the other. My chief job was to carry the food from Canteen 1 to the hospital, their meal times were at 8am, 12.30pm, 4pm and 6pm and the distance was about $1/2$ a mile. Later when the barbed wire was put all around the typhus area the distance was doubled, it certainly kept the cars out but not the DPs.

Besides food carrying I was the duty truck and at first there was much to be done. The hospital only started the day before we arrived and though the Matron in charge is charming and extremely good to the children, she is amazingly unmethodical. We were short of sheets, towels, soap, combs, clothes, toys, blankets, so all these things I fetched from hospital stores or obtained them by any means. Owing to the language difficulty [...] there were many misunderstandings and I found myself sorting things out with a few words of German. The doctor in charge of this block – one Major Smith – was nothing less that a fairy godmother to the children. Toys – most magnificent toys appeared in truck loads, sweets too and later clothes. Swings and see-saws were erected on the playground, and by the way, if you saw the pictures of the swings in the newspaper, they were *not* erected where the gallows had been; in fact no gallows have been found in the Belsen Camp.

After a week or so the children's hospital took over the next block and all the sick children remained – the well ones moved and fed in the new house. Altogether a much better arrangement. My truck was of course most useful during this operation. I managed to do quite a lot of work inside the hospital, meal-times were always more or less pandemonium and required a little organising, store rooms were chaotic because no doors were locked and the children were just allowed to 'go through' everything. The children were particularly attached to toilet rolls, quite a large consignment arrived and every child had one tucked under its arm for several days.

The muddles were gradually sorted out and the BRC who were helping in the hospital were put into the main hospital. I remained for some days, but was not required when a large stove arrived enabling the staff to do the cooking on the spot. This was much more satisfactory, obviously canteen food for adults was in many ways unsuitable for youngsters.

The 3rd block in this area was a German military hospital, this was evacuated and turned into a maternity hospital. They had to be fed. So now I am no longer attached to the children but I feed the maternity hospital 4 times a day and run many errands for them. At first I helped to settle them in but after several days QAs arrived and everything now runs like clockwork.

Now I am really the duty truck for the BRCS. I have my usual feeding to do and I taxi members of the Unit to and from the hospital at 7.50am, 12.50–2.10 for lunch, sisters who have had the afternoon off return at 4.45 and those having the evening off leave at 5pm, and the last taxi departs from the hospital at 7.50pm. We are now much farther from the Baths so I run a service there too.

Apart from these definite jobs I am at everybody's service. Sometimes I cannot find time to help all those who need it. Kit has the first call on the truck and I usually spend the morning or afternoon with her. In between times I run up to hospital stores for pyjamas or saucepans or drive a doctor to the German hospital outside the camp; or take a German prisoner to Mil. Gov. – he was found behind one of the canteens – or take a patient to the dentist. I organised a bread cutting service but unfortunately the electric machine could not take the strain. I later found a good one and it was running most successfully until it was taken over and the electricity failed. That reminds me of another job – no electricity meant no water – all the canteens and hospitals were crying out for water. I luckily found two RAF water-carts who very kindly did the round – they came again the next day and by that time we had an enormous German water-cart on the rounds as well. I deliver dry food-stuffs to the canteens whenever I have half and hour to spare.

M. E. Ashbury, at LBI

Marjorie Ashbury, *Friends' Relief Service*[11]

NOTES

1. Imperial War Museum, Department of Documents (hereafter IWM DD), 85/38/1.
2. From a speech given at the Inter-Allied Conference, June 1945; IWM DD and the Wellcome Archive, London.
3. IWM Sound Archive 11903/2.
4. IWM DD 91/6/1.
5. IWM Sound Archive 9182/03.
6. IWM Sound Archive 9232/2.
7. IWM Sound Archive, 15441/2.
8. From 'Memories of a Red Cross Mission', Wellcome Library.
9. British Red Cross Archives, AccX/278.
10. From 'Friends' Relief Service – June 1945: Reports on Team 100 at Belsen Camp', IWM DD 93/27/2.
11. From 'Friends' Relief Service – June 1945: Reports on Team 100 at Belsen Camp', IWM DD 93/27/2.

Chapter 4
Adjusting to New Realities

In the first weeks of freedom in the Belsen camp, as we have seen, the emphasis of the liberators' work was on dealing with chaos on a grand scale. The work was urgent and generally speaking there was little time for real reflection or for building personal relationships with the survivors. As time went on, the main camp was cleared of people, and, as relatively stable hospitals were established, we see a change in the emphasis of written eyewitness accounts. Through the letters and memoirs of soldiers and medical personnel we are able to gain an insight not only into the medical priorities and practices in the camp, but also into the psychological and moral issues that challenged all who lived and worked in Belsen.

It is important to remember that the prisoners in Bergen-Belsen were a very diverse group with differing cultural and national backgrounds, war histories and states of physical and mental health. While the majority of prisoners remained in a poor state of health in May 1945, a significant number were beginning to recover strength and assert the individuality and freedom denied to them for so long. Some, as we shall see in the next chapter, organized themselves politically and began to liaise with the British authorities about their future. Others were determined to escape the confines of the camp at the earliest opportunity – sometimes, motivated by revenge, to raid local German farms and villages and sometimes in order to link up with groups of fellow nationals liberated nearby.

The behaviour of all survivors – and also that of their colleagues – came under the close scrutiny of British observers and was the subject of much concerned conjecture, particularly by those with a strong religious faith. Although language difficulties often limited communication between liberator and liberated, British personnel began to recognize the psychological impact on their patients of the Nazi crimes and tried to alter their daily practices to gain the trust of people and allay their fears. Thousands of the prisoners in Belsen had recently lived through the reality of Auschwitz, where murderers dressed as doctors, syringes carried lethal injections and chimneys were associated with mass death by asphyxiation. Understandably, in a weakened state, many of the liberated recoiled from medical staff and were unable to accept that the Nazis no longer controlled their fate. This was a difficult situation for the medical personnel to negotiate, particularly as they were working in conditions that made it difficult to give individual patients much personal attention.

Some doctors were able to build up personal relationships, and no one more so than the renowned Irish paediatrician Robert Collis. Working as a member of the Red Cross, he took responsibility for the 500 children in Belsen. Together with the former inmates who had valiantly tried to care for the youngsters under the Kramer regime, he and fellow Red Cross staff nursed the children, who together represented nine nationalities. They slowly built up the trust of the children and learned their tragic stories. Han Hogerzeil, also of the Red Cross, wrote of two brothers and their sister: 'Their father was a Slovak Jew but their mother was a Seventh Day Adventist from Hungary. She wouldn't give the father up so they were all taken here. Their small baby died on the cattle trucks on the way and the mother died on the day of liberation. Their father was murdered.' Collis himself wrote of Belsen in an article published in the *British Medical Journal*:

> The Children's Blocks are the happiest in the whole camp. Many of the children are emaciated...and many are sick; but also many are now beginning to recover, and strange though it may seem, these, particularly the children under 7, do not show the terror symptoms which are perhaps the most terrible aspect of the adult patients' mental state. Already they are laughing and smiling again. Many are going to recover altogether. But our responsibility will not end then, for most have no homes to go to, no parents, no ordinary future. Surely somewhere in the world there are people who will come forward and care for these children and give them a home again.[1]

Indeed, Collis and Hogerzeil, who married after the war, themselves adopted three of the Belsen children.

The future of all the former prisoners, not only the children, concerned our chroniclers. From the perspective of May 1945, while observing the lawlessness of some survivors and the erratic behaviour of others, it was difficult to imagine that the majority would go on to recover their health and leave Germany, to make new lives, to have families and to make a successful living.

To begin with, the terror syndrome was one of the most difficult things with which we had to contend. Most of the children were terrified if we tried to do any medical examinations, and even the tuberculin scratch tests caused panic. Gradually, however, we got their confidence and they began to regard us as their allies and friends.

Robert Collis and Han Hogerzeil[2]

We watch the people here (who are all very kind to us) with rather pitiless eyes because there is one thing in particular that we have learned in the concentration camps: how to get to know people and judge them for their true worth. Most people who should have shown themselves to be human in the hour of need have turned out to be animals. I immediately visualize everybody we meet now as camp inmates and try to imagine how they would behave in such a situation...

Renate Lasker-Wallfisch, *survivor of Auschwitz and Belsen*[3]

Those working in the hospital area on patients who had been removed some weeks previously, patients who had by that time experience of what we were trying to do for them, found it was impossible to give a patient who had any strength an intravenous injection, such as a blood transfusion. The patient was so convinced that she was being given some poison such as benzene as an experiment that she would struggle and scream the place down.

We moved some patients to the German Military Hospital when we had cleared it of the Bosch. As the patients were being unloaded from the ambulances prior to being taken into the wards they started to shout and scream. It was only when we realised that as the doors of the ambulances were opened they could see the tall chimney of the hospital laundry. The poor devils were convinced that they were being taken to the crematorium and we had, in fact, to change our traffic circuit to avoid the mental anguish which that chimney caused.

[...]

It was shortly after the BRCS [British Red Cross Section] teams arrived, though it may have no connection, that a very large quantity of lipstick also arrived. This was not at all what we men wanted. We were screaming for hundreds and thousands of other things and I don't know who asked for lipstick. I wish so much that I could discover who did it. It was the action of genius, sheer unadulterated brilliance. I believe nothing did more for those internees than the lipstick. Women lay in bed with no sheets and no nightie but with scarlet lips. You saw them wandering about with nothing but a blanket over their shoulders, but with scarlet lips. I saw a woman dead on the post mortem table and clutched in her hand was a piece of lipstick.

Do you see what I mean? At last someone had done something to make them individuals again. They were someone, no longer merely the number tattooed on the arm. At last they could take an interest in their appearance. That lipstick started to give them back their humanity.

Perhaps it was the most pathetic thing that happened at Belsen, perhaps the most pathetic thing that has ever happened, I don't know. But that is why the sight of a piece of lipstick today makes my eyes feel just a little uncomfortable.

Lieutenant-Colonel M. W. Gonin, *Commanding Officer,*
11 Light Field Ambulance, RAMC[4]

Dinner-time now was like feeding-time in the Zoo. The children waited breathlessly in bed and waved their spoons. One put on as much as ten pounds in one week! And as they ate so they became happy and laughter filled the place. The terror vanished in conscious form and they seemed altogether happy on the surface. People seeing them then said that of all the people the children had suffered least mentally, but later we found Günther Goldbroch drawing the Long Gallows at Lublin in a book, and another little Dutch boy, aged five, was heard to say when asked where he had last seen his father, 'Hanging by his tie from the door!' Who, therefore, will say how these children will behave in later life, what images of terror they will have hidden in their subconscious minds, which later will bind their minds or harry them?

[...]

Next to food, clothing was of the utmost importance. As long as they had to wear the striped pyjamas, which had been the sole prison garb allowed by the Germans, they felt and indeed looked debased. It was quite hard to realise that the creature whom you saw limping, or staggering out into the sunshine, wearing a dirty blue-and-white-striped, ill-fitting prison garment, was in fact a normal human creature. But, dress her up in a new smart frock, give her a lipstick and some powder and everything was changed. She walked differently, held herself up, carried her head high and now you saw before you a pretty girl. Hence, the clothing of the people was one of the most important measures of all.

Robert Collis and Han Hogerzeil[5]

[Letter dated 4 May 1945]
It is a heartening sight how some of the women 'pick up', i.e. start caring for their dress etc. I only realised to-day – when checking accommodation in Camp 3 and various houses, where girls employed at laundry and various messes are billeted, how pretty many of the girls look – still – or again. They keep their rooms spotlessly clean, there are flowers on the table, and the best sign of all – they flirt with the tommies! If any proof was required that they are gaining self-respect again, this is it. However, I think the number of girls who will definitely become again useful members of human society, will remain small, and still larger than the number of men. I think that 90% of the men will never be able to adjust themselves to civil (and legal) convention. But how can one preach morals to these people, after all they had to go through?

[Letter dated 11 May 1945]

It was again a most wonderful day, almost too warm, like July rather than May. This weather is so beneficial for our internees – they spread all over the beautiful grounds, woods and meadows of this Camp. Even the Typhus cases are sitting half naked – many of them still living skeletons – on their window sills and are enjoying the sun. On the main streets of this part of the Camp they are promenading – thousands of girls, and, in lesser numbers of course, the troops.

It looks like 'mating season' – and it probably is. However, this reminds me again of a more serious problem. It is certainly most wonderful that the girls start feeling at ease in male company, take pride in their appearance, and enjoy life, at least its more emotional aspects. But, I'm afraid, it is going too far. I can very well understand the bottled up feelings of a girl, which makes her throw herself at any man, who treats her gently and doesn't maltreat, nor try to rape her. I can also understand that a tommy – sex-starved as he is here in Germany – wouldn't say 'No.' I have overheard tommies telling each other that most of the girls were probably brought here because they were prostitutes, and that the biggest prostitutes had the best chance of survival and to keep as fit as many girls appear to be now. It all rather upsets me, this entirely wrong interpretation of the girls' behaviour, but I just don't know what could be done about it. Perhaps the Rev. Leslie Hardman should try a bit of persuasion, at least amongst the best types of girls, in addition to the immense practical work he is doing now (which actually has nothing to do with chaplaincy)?

Dr Arnold R. Horwell[6]

Yesterday our CMP [Military Police] checked some of the internees returning to Camp with loot. We just wanted to find out *what* they are looting (as we cannot prevent it). Two little Polish boys (Jewish) of about 12 and 14 respectively, shlepped an enormous bag. We made them empty it – it contained various food stolen from farms, but also a marble chimney-piece clock and some other stuff. Mich asked them, whether they didn't know that they must not steal. So the older one started, waving his hand: 'Stehlen? Wir stehlen doch nicht, wir nehmen doch nur was wir haben, wollen!' [Steal? We aren't stealing, we're just taking what we want]. Well, how can you teach such children morals?

Russian ex-POWs are now taking over guard of this Camp; they are being armed. I don't dare to put on paper what I think will come out of it. Already now we are inundated by cries of help of the remaining civ[ilian] population. I don't think there is a girl left over 14 who hasn't been raped yet on some of these farms around here. I said so often, there is no graver problem facing us than the DP problem. One surely has not too much sympathy with the

German people; but this sort of punishment – well, as Col. Bird expressed it, 'it is so untidy'.

Dr Arnold R. Horwell

There was a great deal of looting in the early days after the liberation. I admit that I joined one of the looting parties myself one day, though I found the experience far from exhilarating. I remember finding myself in a house belonging to some Germans, the general idea being to help oneself to whatever took one's fancy. There was a child in the house who looked at me with total incomprehension. It made me realise that a thief is a thief whatever the circumstances. I left without touching a thing. There could never be adequate compensation for the losses we had sustained. Looting was not the answer.

Anita Lasker-Wallfisch, survivor of Auschwitz and Belsen[7]

245540 Lieut C. H. W. Hodges
Essex Regt
Defence Corp
102 Control Section
BLA

20 May 45

To my parents,

At last I've got some sort of definite job, and, censorship being a thing of more or less nought I can tell you about it.

On Wednesday night, with two of the other ex-gunners and a captain, plus a body of chaps, I arrived at the notorious Belsen Camp. As you see, we are acting as Defence Corp, but I have been given two jobs on my own – Welfare Officer and Prosecuting Officer, which I admit sounds like running with the hare and hunting with the hounds. However, I think I'll shortly be able to hand over the prosecuting to the Military Government people, who should be doing it, which will leave me only the Welfare, which is quite a job in itself in a community of more than 25,000 ex-concentration camp prisoners, to say nothing of the various troops and services who are running the place. [...]

The people are perking up quite a lot, and getting back some of their self-respect and decent habits – as they were nearly all reduced to the very lowest level of bestiality by their conditions. They don't do much to help themselves or us, and there is an antisocial minority which will pinch anything it can lay its hands on. [...]

The latter are the ones who give me my prosecuting work mainly. The court sat for the first time yesterday, when we dealt with a Pole and six Russians. These had a Russian liaison officer to speak for them, and what with him and the interpreter, and the witnesses, it was like the League of Nations gone mad, in a room about 12 foot square. We're sitting again tomorrow, but this time I've managed to fix up a largish sort of wooden hall, which will at least give us breathing space, even if we're still rivalling Babel. I find my French and German are improving from the sheer necessity to make myself understood!

The Welfare work so far has been mainly dealing with cigarettes, books etc., which are sent in, and arranging cinema shows for troops and inmates. This afternoon I got two of the Red Cross women welfare workers – quite competent ladies – and an officer from the Psychological Warfare Section, and we're going to get working on coordination of welfare, and the setting up of information centres etc. in the various camps. I aim at making myself the clearing house for information, ideas, complaints and so on, and at being the link between the Army organisation and the Red Cross etc. work. So I shall be quite glad to get rid of the legal work, though it promises to be interesting. At any rate it's nice to have something definite to do, even if it means a sixteen hour day.

[…]

Cecil.

Lieutenant C. H. W. Hodges, 102 Control Section[8]

We had quite an amusing journey this evening. A Russian girl informed me where there was an excellent electric head cutter in a German canteen, so I told the major and he, a sergeant, the Russian girl and myself all went off to loot it. Unfortunately, we discovered that it was too large to put in the car, so we have to make a further expedition tomorrow with the truck. In Germany anything you want you just go and take, so the looting both necessary and otherwise is terrific. I met the major in charge of loot at a party and he is a most useful attachment as through him I have furnished my kitchens and canteens. I must say that the static equipment is marvellous but everything moveable had been taken, so that there was not even a knife in any of them until I went scrounging. One's whole existence here is absolutely different to anything you could possibly believe and the tales one hears from the few English or French speaking people are absolutely hair raising.

*Miss Margaret Wyndham Ward, British Red Cross Society,
letter of 11 May 1945*[9]

Towards the end, when all fear had completely disappeared, we tried to introduce some disciplinary measures – particularly for the older children. It was excessively difficult to get them to do what they were told or to keep them in bed. Sometimes one who was suffering from tuberculosis, would slip out of bed and disappear for hours. Han found the best way to deal with them was to put them in an isolation ward for a specified time, and take away their clothes. But even so the task of getting them to understand that rules are made to be kept, and that orders must be obeyed, and that it is not a *good thing* to lie and pinch, had to be left, very largely, to the future. We felt indeed that somebody was going to have a very difficult time at some future date and would need much patience and love, if these children were ever to be fitted again into normal society.

Robert Collis and Han Hogerzeil[10]

[B]oth of us carrying the Blessed Sacrament, Fr. Morrison took me round the concentration camp, but this being my first visit it was necessary to be dusted with DDT before leaving the garrison. In a small room in the barracks area a friendly French survivor was voluntarily on duty, ready and happy to protect anyone who had occasion to go into the disease-ridden camp. He had squirted some of the powder up my sleeves, around my ankles, down my neck and under my chin, when he suddenly noticed that under my tunic I was wearing a stole. 'Oh are you a priest?' He asked in surprise. And then for fifteen to twenty minutes he gave a graphic description of the outrageous treatment they had all received and the atrocious sufferings and degradation to which they had been submitted.

Never more will we want to doubt the existence of Hell. As St. Thomas saw and felt our Redeemer's Sacred Wounds so with our very eyes we have seen Hell. Yes with those very eyes I myself have seen Hell. Our languages are not able to express what we have been through. We talk of men, of sub-humans and of sub-beasts, but even this term falls utterly short in its description of the bestialities and degradation to which we have been submitted. Brutality at the hands of the SS and the Gestapo has been the same in every camp of concentration. And for every person you see in this place alive you may reckon 80% were thrown into the incinerators at Auschwitz. See this number tattooed on my arm. This number only gives the thousands. They have left out the number of millions for people were murdered wholesale. Even the women were stripped periodically and examined, and if those between 18 and 30 were too thin or weak to work any more, they were sorted out and thrown into the incinerators half an hour later. No spiritual administration was ever allowed in the camps; all hope was beaten out of us; we were debased and degraded beyond human belief. In every camp it was the same. Therefore, if we who have suffered

𝔗𝔥𝔢 𝔖𝔞𝔵𝔬𝔫 𝔠𝔥𝔲𝔯𝔠𝔥

at

𝔅𝔯𝔢𝔞𝔪𝔬𝔯𝔢

Date: C. 980 A.D.

Notice to Visitors

Funds are urgently required for the upkeep of the Fabric of this church. The price of this pamphlet is ⬤ Pence. *25*

Please take one and place your contribution in the box provided for that purpose.

Breamore Church, Hampshire

By ARTHUR R. GREEN, F.S.A.,
Author of "Sundials, Incised Dials or Mass Clocks"

Visitors' attention is particularly directed to the
following facts:

Breamore is a **Saxon Church,** built about the year A.D. 980,
and the **Saxon features of chief interest** are:

The Tower and Arch into the Transept.

The long and short work of large stones at the angle.

The pilaster strips.

The double-splayed windows.

The Saxon Rood.

BREAMORE VILLAGE lies on the right bank of the
Christchurch Avon on the high road from Fordingbridge
to Salisbury. On the north-east side of the parish lies
Charford, and in connection with the origin of the Kingdom of the
West Saxons the early legends of Wessex tell us that a great battle
was fought here (Cerdicsford) in A.D. 519 by the Saxon invaders
under Cerdic, which ended in the slaughter of 5,000 Britons and
their King, Natan-Leod, who, according to local tradition, is
buried in the Long Barrow on Breamore Down, on the Whitsbury
side of the Miz-Mase, near Grim's Ditch.

About half a mile from the village stands the church,
picturesquely situated, surrounded by beautiful trees, in Breamore
Park.

HISTORICAL. From the years 980 to 1130 information
about Breamore Church is scanty. Who built it or how it was
administered during that period is the subject of further research.
With the founding of the Augustine Priory in 1130 there is a very
complete history of the successive priors who administered the
church. A full account is set out in the Victoria History of Hampshire, Vols. 2 and 4.

In 1536 Thomas Cromwell, as the king's agent, appointed a
Commission of Visitors to the Monasteries to give colour to their
confiscation. In the account of 30th May, 1536, not a single
scandal is even hinted at in connection with the Hampshire
Houses, the report on the Austin canons of Breamore was "that
they are of good conversion." Notwithstanding the nature of these
reports every one of the smaller houses was suppressed before the

close of the year. Prior Finch was, on 21st June, 1536, assigned a pension of £18 per annum, and in March, 1538, he was made Suffragan bishop of Taunton. The site of the Priory was granted to Henry Marquis of Exeter and Gertrude his wife, together with all its possessions, amongst which is enumerated the Manor of Breamore and the rectories and chapels of Breamore. The site of the Priory can still be seen adjoining the River Avon and North of Breamore Mill. Excavations on the site in 1898 revealed only traces of the cloisters and some stone coffins, three of which were removed and placed beside the old Yew tree in Breamore Church-yard to preserve them from damage. Some beautiful old tiles found during the excavations can be seen in Salisbury Museum.

BREAMORE CHURCH is a large and handsome structure and is of special interest, being a valuable and practically complete example of a Saxon building dating from late in the Xth or early in the XIth century. It is exceptionally long (96ft 6in) and consists of a chancel and aisle-less nave, separated by a square central tower, from which there opened originally a lateral porticus or chapel or transept on each side, the one on the north having now disappeared, and there are indications that a western adjunct also existed opening into and of the same width as the nave.

The walls are composed of whole flints with large quoins of irregular long and short work and pilaster strips of green sand-stone and ironstone, but the appearance it now presents is very different to its original aspect, for the whole church both within and without was covered in pre-conquest times with plaster, the only portions left uncovered being the quoins and pilaster strips, which projecting from the face of the wall are cut back to receive it, but it is continued unbroken over the splays of the windows. Alterations have been few, but the chancel was re-built in the XIVth century, the old walls in their lower part being retained, and a south porch has been added.

Breamore is not, strictly speaking, a cruciform church, but its most interesting architectural feature is that it presents a step forward in the evolution of the cruciform or cross plan (which eventually became such a prominent feature in mediaeval church construction in England), with the tower between the nave and chancel resting on piers and arches, the latter opening to transepts of the same width as the tower, the whole connected together in one structure. In some of the earlier churches there had been side chapels (porticus), as for instance as St Pancras, Canterbury, where they projected from the side of the nave, half-way up its length. In latter churches, such as Britford, near Salisbury, and Deerhurst, Gloucestershire, the chapels projected on each side near the east end of the nave.

At Worth, in Sussex, the plan is unmistakable cruciform, with partially developed transepts projecting from the eastern part of the nave, but there is no original tower. At Breamore a distinct advance is made—the quoins of the tower, which is one of the same width as the nave are carried to the ground, while internally a square space is formed between the nave and the chancel, the side walls of which are pierced by narrow archways which lead into a lateral chapel. These lateral adjuncts are not real transepts, they are narrower than the tower and their roof-line is lower than the nave, and still more important, they do not act as abutments to the central tower, which was essential in the fully developed cruciform plan, but they represent a step forward towards its planning and construction.

THE CHANCEL was rebuilt in the XIVth century, but probably the lower parts of the wall belong to the original Saxon Church. The east window, with its reticulated or net-like tracery, dates from about 1340. On each side of it is an **IMAGE BRACKET** of XVth century date, ornamented with angel heads and foliage. The one on the north no doubt supported an image of the Virgin Mary, and the one on the south perhaps St Michael, the dedication of the church being to St Mary, but formerly to St Mary and St Michael.

The north wall has no windows, but externally, towards the west end, there are traces—part of the sill and one jamb—of one of those curious openings to which the name **"LOW SIDE WINDOW"** has been given. Popularly, but mistakenly, they are called "Leper Windows", and although many theories have been advanced none of them can claim to explain the purpose for which all of them were originally constructed. The theories which receive the greatest support from ecclesiologists at the present time are: (1) The Sanctus Bell Theory, which suggests that "low side windows" were for the purpose of ringing a hand-bell through, at appropriate time during Mass, so that people who were unable to be present at the service might take notice and bend their knees, and (2) The Confessional Theory, which suggests that these openings were for hearing confessions through, the penitent being outside and the priest inside the church.

In the south wall a XVth century **PICINA** in a niche, which originally was closed by a door, one hinge pin of which still remains, and above are two recesses for cruets. To the west of this are a window and priest's door dating from about 1340, and a XVth century window. Externally, the original weather table shows that the early chancel roof was of about the same height as that of the nave and the original walls much higher than they are now.

The **CHANCEL ARCH** and the arch in the west wall of the tower were inserted early in the XVth century in the place of the original Saxon arches. They are now as wide as the chancel and are stopped on bands of foliage and supported on capitals, short wall-shafts, and corbels with beautiful foliage, and one with a human head. The foliage is peculiar—thistle leaves, oak leaves and acorns, and vine leaves and grapes are all represented, and the sculpture evidently belongs to the same school as the work at Christchurch Priory.

A ROOD-LOFT formerly stood across the western arch, and its upper door-way with its old wooden frame, can still be seen on the north side. Rood-lofts were ordered to be removed in Edward VIth reign (1548), and in the place formerly occupied by the Rood the Royal Arms was set up, but the **ROYAL ARMS** now present here are later and date from the XVIIIth century, and those used by George I, II and III. The west wall of the **NAVE** has been re-built, but in the lower part of the jambs of the original door-way which opened into the destroyed western chamber can still be seen, and also, under the diagonal buttresses, the start of the walls of the chamber. On the right-hand side of the south door, inside the church, is a niche for the **HOLY WATER STOUP. The FONT** is ancient, but of uncertain date.

THE CENTRAL TOWER originally had a floor of 15 feet from the ground from which the bells were rung; this has disappeared and the bells are now rung from the ground floor. The entrance to this upper roof was from the south transept by a narrow square-headed doorway and a ladder or a wooden stairway. The upper part of the tower is a curved timber structure as seen from the inside, and externally it may well represent a Saxon original. The north transept has disappeared, but the weathering on its roof can be seen on the north wall externally, and the lower part of the blocked jambs of the archway leading to it.

THE SOUTH TRANSEPT or chapel remains, and the archway leading to it is of more than ordinary interest. The wall in which it is placed is three feet thick, and the arch, semi-circular in shape, is of one square order, the voussoirs being "through" stones. The jambs support massive square abaci, with a large cable moulding on the angles, a somewhat rare ornament in the Anglo-Saxon period.

An inscription in Anglo-Saxon is incised on the north face of the arch, which reads as follows:

"HER SWUTELATH SEO GECWYDRAEDNES THE."
This may be translated—

"Here is made p'ain (is manifested) the covenant (the word)
to thee," which would seem to be a quotation from Titus i, 3:
"But God hath in due time manifested to us His Word."

The sentence may have been completed elsewhere, possibly upon the three corresponding arches now destroyed; indeed there is one other stone preserved in the wall which bear the letters "DES."

From the form of the letters, it seems certain that the inscription must date from the latter part of the reign of Ethelred II, 979-1016.

SAXON WINDOWS. Seven of these remain, and they are characteristic of the late Saxon period, being "double-splayed", with the actual aperture for light at about the middle of the thickness of the wall and having a splay both outwards and inwards. They are round-headed, and their jambs, which slope outwards, are comprised of flint rubble covered with plaster. There are three on the first floor of the tower, but they have all been altered and have now square-headed stone frames externally. The south-east window has been destroyed. In the south transept is one of these windows, complete and unaltered. It is on the east, above a XIIth century door-way, and on the south is another, but a pointed XIIth century lancet has been inserted into its outer splay. On the north side of the nave, placed high in the wall, are two more original windows, and there is another blocked up, and now partly hidden by the porch in the south wall.

The other windows of the church date from the XIVth, XVth and XVIth centuries. The large west window is modern, and over it is set a shield, on which is carved the letters W.D. and the date 1603, no doubt the initials of Sir William Dodington, the then Lord of the Manor. On the west side of the south transept is a XVth century window, carved on a shield on the west dripstone is a besant between two harts' heads cabossed in chief quartering a chevron between roundels, which is perhaps a Popham coat quartered with Zouche. In the transept there is a print from Hart MSS., fo. 420576, of Sir John Popham Knight, who lived at Charford. He belonged to the knightly family of Popham, of Popham, near Micheldever, and was Treasurer of the Household of King Henry VI, and died in 1463.

THE PORCH which covers the south doorway is of very great interest. It is of two dates, the lower portion being erected in the middle of the XIIth century, to which time the south door-way belongs, and the upper part was added in the XVth century. The half-timbered gable is modern. The upper chamber, the floor of which has been removed, was no doubt constructed like the similar chamber at the west end of Headbourne Worthy Church, to do honour to, and to preserve the rood. It is decorated with wall-paintings, and the piscina belonging to its altar still remains, as also the stone corbels inside the porch which would have carried the main beams supporting the floor.

THE SAXON ROOD, with figures of Our Lady and St John, has been dreadfully mutilated by some miscreant, but enough remains to show what a striking sculpture it must have been in its original state. It may be compared with similar sculptural pieces at Headbourne Worthy and Romsey, and in all these there is, above the head of the Crucified Saviour, the Manus Dei (the Hand of God) projecting downwards from a cloud. The frescoes, in brown, blue and black colours, are noteworthy, and form a background to the three figures. A rolling landscape is depicted with a church and other buildings, and trees and woods and the sacred monogram I.H.S. and the letters A.B.M., "Ave beata Maria" ("Hail blessed Mary"), are faintly visible. On the western side the hanging figure of Judas can be seen. Below the paintings are continued on the east and west walls, where the rood is a XIIth century circular medallion containing an **AGNUS DEI** (Lamb of God), carved in low relief.

THE BENCHES in the porch were made by a local carpenter from the original steps and rails leading to the old belfry in the tower; and the date 1617 on one of them applies to the steps and not to the bench.

MASS CLOCKS. A Mass clock is an early kind of sundial which we often find incised on the walls of ancient churches; they are always incomplete, the pointer or gnomen having been lost. Before clocks were invented they no doubt told the time for the time of the church services, especially the time of Mass. There are three Mass clocks here: one a very small dial, at the west angle of the porch, and two others on quoins at the south-east angle of the transept.

THE BELLS. There are four bells, and each bears an inscription and date and the initials of the founder:

Treble: "Seek God." J.W., 1604.
Second: "Fear God." J.W., 1613.
Third: "Give God the Glory." J.W., 1591.
Tenor: "O sing praise unto God." J.D., 1629.

They were cast in Salisbury by John Wallis, a well-known bell-founder of that city, and by John Danton, who succeeded him. They were recast in 1922 by Messrs. Taylor and Sons, of Loughborough, much of the original metal being used.

THE ROOFS. The nave roof contains some old material re-used, but the chancel roof is modern.

Printed by W. E. Collins Ltd. Ferndown Industrial Estate. Wimborne. Dorset so much behave like the old Romans, take some Germans and pitch them and burn them like torches in public on our victory night, you need not be surprised...

[...]

After conducting me round the concentration camp in the morning of May 15th Fr. Morrison also introduced me to some of those with whom I would be working during my short stay, and explained the general situation of the personnel in the garrison and hospital blocks. Going round this camp in the afternoon, and passing 'Harrods', the huts serving as clothing stores, we unexpectedly met a Polish priest. It would appear that he had been searching for a hat or cap to match his very unclerical dress, and that presumably he was one of the few priests to survive from the Horror Camp. He was a Fr. Konopka SJ, one time Provincial of the Polish Province. He spoke to us rapidly and at great length in fluent Latin, and I can only regret that the composition of the place prevented my paying greater attention to what he wanted us to remember. And I never saw him again. However one phrase repeated frequently could not fail to stick in the mind. 'Nota bene, Pater, nota bene...' [note well, Father, note well]. And now having the opportunity to note everything around him it was easy to guess that he was answering many unspoken questions, who, when, why, what for, how long, where? etc.

[...]

I joined Fr. Fay and L'Abbé Morvillez in the task of visiting the hospital patients and administering Holy Communion and Viaticum to the sick and dying. A young French man, a member of the Jocist movement, accompanied me whenever I was carrying the Blessed Sacrament to the patients. He kept ahead of me to enquire who were Catholics in each room, and asked them to prepare for the priest who was bringing Our Lord to them. He was then able to conduct me to a room and point out who were, or who were not, Catholic, and while I was attending to them, he would be making enquiries in the next room, or calling my attention to someone who appeared to be near to dying. His co-operation was very valuable because many of the Jews thought the priest was simply giving out some sort of medicine to which they were equally entitled. For example, one day in a small room where I had just given Holy Communion to a patient near the window, I overheard conversations behind my back. My guide had returned for me, and a Jewish patient in bed near the door was trying to explain to him that he also would like some vitamins. He was given an expressive reply. 'Nicht vitamins hier' (pointing to his stomach); 'Vitamins hier', indicating his head.

Reverend Father Edmund Swift, S. J., *Roman Catholic Chaplain to 81 British General Hospital*[11]

Rev. I. Levy, S.C.F.
Rear HQ Second Army
BLA

1st June 1945

To all ranks of the Jewish Faith,

No doubt a large number of you have been asking the old question 'What has happened to the Jewish chaplains and why have we not seen them for so many weeks?' Several complaints have actually reached me that the chaplains have not 'been doing their stuff' lately.

The purpose of this circular therefore is to clear the air and to bring to your notice a number of points which I know will be of interest.

The name of Belsen Concentration Camp had been on everyone's lips since it was liberated some six weeks ago. It is the largest camp in Germany from the view point of its Jewish inmates. When the chaplains arrived there shortly after it was liberated we found some 20,000–25,000 Jews there. The last relics of European Jewry. Their condition was too appalling to bear description. Need I therefore assure you that they have claimed pride of place in our affection and attention. As you know there were only two Jewish Chaplains in 2nd Army Area and one serving with the British increment of the Canadian Army. To whom were we to devote our attention to the soldiers who, thank God, were healthy or to these poor unfortunates for whom we brought the first Jewish greeting they had heard in years? You know the answer.

But with the elimination of that Hell camp we are still faced with the problem of serving those who have survived. Throughout the British zone of occupation we have found groups and camps containing Jewish victims. All of them require our aid and spiritual and physical attention. I am sure that we are voicing your sentiments in this direction too. You would not want us to do anything else, I am certain. We came to Europe to liberate the oppressed and we have found our long lost brethren.

The time has now come when you can help us too. You may find groups of Jews in the areas in which you are serving. Contact them in our name and give them comfort. Collect their names and first names, the date of their birth and place of origin and send me the information. This is invaluable in that thereby we may help to trace their families. Would you like to make some material contribution too? We want to give them comforts which will help them to maintain their morale during the period of waiting for repatriation. The men need just those things which you would need in the army. Cigarettes, sweets, chocolates, tooth brushes and tooth paste etc., etc. You can participate in this work by sending any contribution you care to make to me and I shall be happy to deliver it to the people who need it so much. By this gesture you can feel that you too are helping to alleviate their suffering. I shall not thank you for it since I know you will not ask for gratitude. The knowledge that one helps is its own reward.

May the day of their complete liberation soon come and with it the end of their long and bitter suffering.

Best wishes to you all,
I. Levy, S.C.F.
Senior Jewish Chaplain.

Reverend I. Levy, SCF[12]

There was one lady in the block where I worked, and she was a Polish Jew, and she could speak excellent English – which was really such a blessing! So we used to have quite long chats together, and she said 'I hope when all this is finished that we will be able to get to America.' And I said 'That would be marvellous, and I hope that when you're there you will tell everybody about this place.' And she said 'Well, no, I've told my daughter not to talk about it.' And I said, 'Oh, you must tell them about this.' And she said 'no, because first of all, they said nobody will want to know, and secondly, nobody would be interested.' And to a certain extent, she was really right, that people after the war weren't really interested in what went on in Germany then.
[. . .]

I could talk about it [when I returned], especially to the family. But as this lady said, most people don't want to know about it. And if they did know, they wouldn't believe it. And I found that that was very true after the war – they didn't want to hear about it.

Norrie Alexander, *British Red Cross*[13]

[From letter dated Thursday 17th May 1945]
During the show a fat, well dressed fellow came over to me and introduced himself as the manager of the cinema across the field. As this cinema was being run by 'Welfare' I was not sure how to answer him, until he told me that his wife's sister was Marlene Dietrich. I left him abruptly. I was in no mood to talk to Germans after what I'd seen, even if their sisters were Hedy Lamour and Betty Grable.
[. . .]

From tragedy to entertainment and the evening show. The hall was already half filled with Russians, Poles, Czechs, Hungarians, and representatives of at least six other countries. I did not know the time so looked for someone with a watch. Just behind me were two Russian girls wearing wristlet watches, and I asked them in that wonderful language of gesture and facial expression what time it was. They held out their arms so that I could see their watches; but I saw more than the watches – their numbers had been tattooed into the skin. In case you should wonder how they should possess watches, I should add that the watches have been acquired since their release; but that is another story.

Well, the film 'Babes on Broadway', plus a musical 'short' was very well received, and even during the dialogue, which must have been very monotonous and uninteresting to them, all was quiet, save for an occasional whisper in a strange tongue commenting to a neighbour on something unusual in custom or dress.

And so another day nears an end. The equipment is packed up, a few more lines added to this letter, followed by a thorough wash down and 'dusting', and so to bed and sleep if the struggles of a horror wracked mind will permit.

Before closing I should clear up a point that may be confusing. The cinema show was held, not in Belsen Camp proper, but in the larger camp known as Belsen which is in actual fact the SS Barracks and Bergen Camp, which adjoin the real Belsen. As I have mentioned, the destruction has already begun of the horror camp, and the widespread plague of Typhus would make such a show impossible.

[From letter dated Tuesday 12 June 1945]

[. . .]

People who two months ago were living an animal existence are living like true human beings again and taking an interest in themselves. This, I think, has been one of the medical corps finest jobs.

[. . .]

As I told you, concerts, in which the inmates are also the stars, are being run, and many other social entertainments have been arranged. Also an educational corps sergeant with whom I am very friendly has opened up a school which is very successful.

Yesterday I was standing outside a hospital office when an ambulance drove up. In it were about a dozen women all looking very excited and clasping in their arms the precious bundle of clothes with which they had just been issued. One or two had already put their new shoes on and walked along very carefully, and obviously finding great difficulty in keeping their balance.

But their excitement and happiness was a real tonic. No women coming from a sale with a hard won bargain could have looked more triumphant; no child wearing its mother's high-heeled shoes could have looked prouder. And these two examples were the very ones that flashed through my mind as I saw them.

Just two bed statements outside the hospital wards I read, on both was written 'Deaths – nil'.

Now, I have spoken a lot in praise of the RAMC, and there is nothing too high I can say for the splendid work they have done. Yet all here agree that the hardest working and most energetic body in the whole of Belsen are – the German nurses. These girls have done remarkable things and the medical orderlies declare that they put the English sisters to shame. When the German nurses came to Belsen they were treated disgustingly – not by the British – yet in spite of this they have worked like true nurses – and more!

I mention these nurses because they do deserve mention and you will read nothing of them in the papers.

There are always plenty of celebrities visiting Belsen and today's visitor was Mary Churchill. On Thursday, four top line stars are giving a play to the staff at Belsen; two of them are Dame Sybil Thorndyke and Laurence Olivier.

C. J. Charters, 37 Kinema Section RAOC, BLA[14]

NOTES

1. W. R. F. Collis, 'Belsen Camp: A preliminary report', *British Medical Journal*, 9 June 1945, pp. 814–15.
2. Robert Collis and Han Hogerzeil, *Straight On* (London: Methuen & Co. Ltd, 1947), pp. 63–4.
3. Anita Lasker-Wallfisch, *Inherit the Truth 1939–1945* (London: Giles de la Mare, 1996), pp. 111–12.
4. Imperial War Museum, Department of Documents (hereafter IWM DD), 85/38/1.
5. Collis and Hogerzeil, *Straight On*, pp. 71–3.
6. IWM DD, 91/21/1.
7. Lasker-Wallfisch, *Inherit the Truth 1939–1945*, pp. 108–9.
8. IWM DD (no ref. no.) This testimony appears with changes made by the author.
9. British Red Cross Archives, AccX/278.
10. Collis and Hogerzeil, *Straight On*, p. 147.
11. IWM DD 90/4/1.
12. IWM DD, Misc. 180, Item 2719.
13. IWM Sound Archive, 15441/2.
14. IWM Docs, Con. Shelf.

Chapter 5
Belsen as a Jewish Displaced Persons' Camp

Since 1945, the name Belsen has been synonymous for most people only with horror and degradation. The second phase of its almost ten-year history,[1] and in particular the years between 1946 and 1948, are less documented and widely discussed. During this time, following the establishment of a Jewish Displaced Persons' (DP) Camp in the former Wehrmacht barracks, the site became a symbol of the 'rebirth' and rehabilitation of the Jewish people. At the local level, it thrived politically, culturally and socially, but on the international stage, too, the spotlight fell on Belsen during the power struggle that led to Britain relinquishing its Mandate in Palestine and the creation of the state of Israel in 1948. (The British renamed the centre Hohne but the Jewish Committee in charge of internal administration rightly judged that Belsen would be a far more powerful propaganda tool, and its members clung fiercely to the name.)

The period immediately after the end of the war saw a huge movement of refugees across Europe. The Allied governments sought to return to their country of origin as quickly as possible all the forced labours, concentration camp victims and other persons displaced by the war. The first premise of the Allied repatriation policy was the belief that all liberated peoples in Europe desired to return home. While this was the case for most French, Dutch and Russians, for example, most Jewish people had absolutely no interest in returning to towns and villages in Poland, Hungary and Germany where entire communities had been murdered and where the local population were hostile. They preferred to remain stateless in DP camps in the West and thus the Jewish DP Camp at Belsen evolved. Some Jewish DPs did leave Belsen in the early months after the war – some to recuperate in Sweden and the lucky ones to live with surviving family members elsewhere abroad. The majority, however, saw no choice but to stay put and hope that quotas for the USA were relaxed or that the gates of Palestine were opened by the British. Their numbers were swelled by other Jews travelling into Germany from the East.

Contemporary estimates place the number of Jews in Belsen in the second half of 1945 at between 10,000 and 12,000. As the largest Jewish community in the British zone it was in a position to wield a significant amount of influence. The Jewish Committee that represented the community was extremely effective in getting its voice heard, not only by the British Military Government on the ground in Germany but by the British and American governments and Jewish communities around the world. It organized early – just weeks after liberation – and made links with other Jewish communities in Germany, holding a conference in September 1945. Collectively, they set their sights on lobbying for an Israeli state. Throughout the post-war years Belsen played host to a great deal of underground activity, not least as a hub in the smuggling of people, goods and weapons into Palestine. On one occasion, when the British decided to make an example of a boat of illegal immigrants they had intercepted on the way to Palestine by turning it back to Europe, some former Belsen residents found themselves at the centre of an international incident known as the *Exodus* affair.

Yet there was more to Belsen than politics. Thousands of people made the site their semi-permanent home in the post-war years and, with the help of overseas aid agencies, such as the British Jewish Relief Unit and the American Jewish Joint Distribution Committee, turned Belsen into a thriving 'town' complete with theatre, cinema, a library and its own newspaper. Couples were married and had children in Belsen; the children went to school. The extracts below give us a flavour of the vibrant day-to-day life in the camp, as well as the frustrations and restrictions that characterized this 'living in limbo'.

*

In the new Höhne Camp the evacuees from Camp 1 were grouped according to their nationalities. The already existing system of National Committees was maintained and improved. The 224 and 618 Mil. Gov. Dets. that were in charge of the camp gave instructions to the Directors of the various Committees, who transmitted them to the block leaders in their particular area. [. . .]

Soon after the liberation a quick repatriation of a maximum of DPs to their own countries became one of the main problems to be dealt with in Belsen.

The westbounders (French, Belgian, Dutch DPs) were, if their physical condition allowed, repatriated within a few weeks starting from the 15th of May. The repatriation of DPs from eastern countries had to be delayed until the war was over and something was known of the conditions prevailing in those countries.

The lists of repatriated DPs were made by the Liaison Officers with the help of the National Committees and copies were handed over to 618 Mil. Gov. Det.

Altogether about 30,000 DPs who had been liberated in Belsen were thus repatriated. Later on more DPs were repatriated from Belsen but these had originally been liberated in other camps.

Lieutenant H. François Poncet, *French Search Officer, Belsen,*
'Report on the Search in Belsen', Belsen, 10 June 1946[2]

My closest friends, Hélène Wiernik, Hélène Rounder and Violette Silberstein, and all the others who had countries to go back to, had left Belsen and gone 'home'. No one had had any idea what they would find on their return but at least they had somewhere to start searching. That was not the case with us. It would not have crossed our minds to consider Germany or Breslau, by then in Russian hands, as our 'home'.

For the record I must mention something here that I have only found out quite recently: it is that Jewish army personnel had a fight on their hands to convince the officers in charge of 'repatriation' that they should not divide the survivors into their respective nationalities and then help them to 'return home'. The complexities for our liberators in sorting out the unprecedented chaos were enormous; but it could not be expected of the average British army officer who had been sent off to fight a war that he should be able to grasp fully the significance of the term 'displaced person'. That was precisely what we were, displaced persons. The question was, where could we be 'placed'?

For the moment we were still in Belsen, and very slowly exchanging our preoccupation with death for a new concern: *life*.

Anita Lasker-Wallfisch, *survivor of Auschwitz and Belsen*[3]

I am taking the liberty of writing to you in order to bring to your notice a number of problems affecting the Jews in the Belsen camp.

I am sure it would be needless to bring to your attention the appalling conditions which we found on our entry into the camp. I have been working there for some time now and I regret to say that even though the military are doing all they can to restore the wretched inmates to physical recovery, their mental anxieties are far from allayed. There are some 20,000 Jews there, and possibly more, whose nationalities vary according to the countries from which they were deported. The vast majority are Eastern Europeans.

It is self evident that the majority of these Jews cannot return to the countries of their origin. They fear a resurgence of the same ideology which brought them to this present impasse. The youth in particular see no future in their former countries. They have orientated their much-dreamed-of future to settlement in Palestine, which is the obvious solution for them. Some desire to return to their countries of origin in the hope that they may find some trace of their families. But this is only a temporary measure. They are determined that their final destination is Palestine.

Meanwhile, the great problem is the immediate future facing them and us. Very shortly the first great exodus from Belsen will take place under the auspices of the Military authorities. The usual DP channels will be brought into play. The evacuees from Belsen will be passed through various camps according to their nationalities. The great 'Drang nach Osten' [desire for expansion eastwards] may be enacted.

I have urged that the Jewish victims of the Nazis deserve special consideration. I feel most strongly that a Jewish Transit Camp should be opened with all possible haste to which all Jews who do not desire to be repatriated should be sent, there to remain until the powers that be can arrive at a decision which will define their status and future. I am sure that organisations such as yours would sympathise with such a suggestion.

I would further suggest that the ideal site for such a Transit Camp is Hanover, where the inmates of the local camp are well organised. I am assured that there is ample accommodation for a considerable number of Jews. There is an excellent agricultural school in the area where youth could be trained for work on the land.

Another problem which faces us is the future of the German Jewish nationals in Belsen. Some of them have already been sent out of the camp with a mere pittance in their pockets. They will now wander over the countryside in the vain attempt to search for their families and a source of livelihood. I see little prospect for such people who have spent so many years in concentration camps. Surely they deserve special consideration.

I appeal to you and to your vast organisation to come to our aid. Can any pressure be brought to bear to expedite the establishment of Jewish Transit Camps? I cannot do more than stress the point with the Military, but they wait for instructions from above – the usual Military procedure. Were an order given they would obey it. From the depths of desperation in Belsen I most earnestly appeal to you to do everything possible to help this last relic of European Jewry.

Reverend Isaac Levy to Mr T. T. Scott of the Displaced Persons Section
of the United Nations Relief and Rehabilitation Administration,
16 May 1945[4]

[From letter dated 15 May 1945]
I gather from your letter that two teams are preparing to come over here: the JCRA [Jewish Committee for Relief Abroad], and the Joint [American Joint Distribution Committee], and you say, it might take another fortnight before they get moving. Well, darling, as things are developing, they will be weeks too late. On May 21st almost all 'fit' internees will leave the Camp, and other transports will leave shortly after, as soon as the internees will be fit enough to travel. Unless, in the last minute, we get our opinion recognised that Jews

should be considered as Jews (according to their choice), and not as members of their various nationalities, it will be most difficult to trace them. There are only two possibilities: (a) either the teams must arrive well before May 21st, with definite authority to sort things out here, or (b) we must get authority through to treat the Jews as different from the DPs of their 'nationality' and send them to special Jewish centres, so that the teams, when it pleases them to arrive here, will be able to find them in Jewish groups – say at Hanover or (you might have read yesterday's Express) in the 'stateless' camp at Lingen. What will be left here after 21st May will be only Hospital cases – approx. 15,000 to 17,000, and your two teams will be hanging around here, with no job to do, unless, of course, they'll decide to travel the country in search for the scattered remnants of Israel. And, heaven knows where they will find their lost tribes – I assure you, there will be more than ten of them.

[From letter dated 16 May 1945]
Belsen Concentration Camp, 16th May 1945

My only dearest love,
Yes, we are allowed now to state our location – so in case you didn't know...
[...]
    And now, dearest, comes Great News: Col. Bird has just been in and congratulated me – 'Horwell, great news for us all, your scheme has been approved by 2nd Army.' It appears that the news released prematurely in the Express was based on facts. After my talk with him, the Staff-Major controlling Civ. Affairs (Mil. Gov.) at 2nd Army drafted a report based on my suggestion. As the 'higher-ups' could not drop the principle of not recognising 'denominations', it was decided to institute a new 'nationality': Stateless. Every DP, everybody in this Camp, who either does not want to return to his country, or, as a Jew, does not want to be bundled together with his Polish or German etc. compatriots, will be given the choice to register as 'stateless', and will be taken to special Jewish transit camps; the first one is being established at Lingen (near Rheine), and will be reserved for the big release next week from Belsen. Reason for not choosing Hanover: Lingen can take up to 8,000.
    All this news came through today – Col. Bird sent up the Senior Mil. Gov. Officer (Col. Spottiswood) to 2nd Army to have it confirmed. I am expecting all sorts of sabotage from Mil. Gov. in the execution of this order (it might involve a bit more work for them), but I am feeling perfectly capable of dealing with this aspect of the business. I shall just get my team of Chaplains busy to broadcast the news amongst the internees. Well, darling, I feel immensely happy about this success, I can count this as one of the greatest days of my life. Once the principle is recognised, it might alter the whole

aspect of Allied Mil. Gov. policy towards the Jewish problem. When Bird congratulated me, he said: 'As usual, when a great thing is achieved, you won't get the credit for it.' And I gladly replied, I certainly did neither do it for personal credit's sake, nor do I wish to minimise his own moral support, nor Levy's great help. But, still, it gives me the greatest possible satisfaction. And there is another aspect of the matter: don't you think that it is grand, that for once the ball started rolling uphill, i.e. that the effort of the most junior officer, the only subaltern of this HQ, should have initiated not only a change of policy on Army HQ level, but also, perhaps, in the principles of Allied DP policy by creating this precedent? I haven't dared yet to think out the further implications, i.e. what is going to happen to those people who mercifully will be spared compulsory repatriation to their hated native countries – I shall tell you my views on this subject another day, hoping that they will fall on as fertile soil as my last initiative. Alas, Anglo-Jewry might be more difficult to tackle than the 2nd Brit. Army, or even Mil. Gov.!

[From letter dated 20 May 1945]
I had called a conference together this morning – the Chaplains and Jane L[evy, who worked for the Red Cross], about the 'Stateless' question. You cannot imagine our difficulties, the Mil. Gov. people never explained to the people concerned that, in order not to be sent back to their countries of origin, they must call themselves stateless. They just register the answer to the question: what nationality? And how few know that they can chose to be stateless! And even fewer know that it would be to their advantage to do so. From another side our intentions are sabotaged as well: The 'liaison' officers of the various nations concerned walk about and tell everybody, if he selects to be stateless he will be sent to Madagascar (or Senegal) right away. Well, this nonsense must stop, and we saw the Mil. Gov. people about it. Now the Chaplains are touring each Block and explain the position, and people who have registered yesterday as Polish etc. are changing their mind. It is a hell of a job!
    [...] Miss Livingstone paid a visit to Col. Bird today – they are very enthusiastic about each other, and both with excellent reason! I just cannot get over it – to have a sympathetic, understanding and truly humane Commander at a place like that. Actually, what he has achieved, is immense – during the 3 weeks of our stay the complete horror Camp was cleaned, 17,000 people hospitalised, the remainder fit to move off, or, if still staying here, staying under comparatively comfortable conditions. And without his moral support, our cause would have failed and we could never have achieved the 'precedent' of recognising our Jewish problem as different from the other DPs.

                                                                    Dr Arnold R, Horwell[5]

In May, when the first parties of Poles left Belsen for the Polish camp of Bardowic, the Jews from Poland were told to choose between going with them or going to a camp at Lingen near the Dutch frontier. They were told that Lingen was a camp for 'stateless persons'. In fact the word 'stateless' was a misnomer, for it signifies the loss of all rights of citizenship, and these Polish Jews had not been deprived of their citizenship by any Polish government. The choice between 'statelessness' and a Polish camp was difficult and harsh, particularly as it had to be made at a few hours' notice. Placed thus before two such alternatives many Jews in Belsen, both men and women, became nervous and distraught, and at this juncture Colonel Bird, the garrison commander, intervened. At a conference, presided over by a senior Military Government Officer, and attended by representatives of the Belsen Jewish Committee, a statement was drawn up making clear to people who were unwilling to return home [to Poland] what their position was.

They learnt that no citizen of the United Nations would be repatriated against his will; that a decision not to be repatriated did not entail loss of the right to choose to be repatriated at a later date; and that the future of people not wishing to return to their homeland would be decided by an international organisation.

This statement still defined the position of the Poles, Jewish and non-Jewish, who remained in Belsen in October, 1945, because of their reluctance to go back to Poland. There were eight thousand of them.

Derrick Sington, Commander of 14 Amplifier Unit,
Intelligence Corps[6]

The Swedish Government arranged, as part of a big relief scheme, to receive seven thousand out of the ten thousand sick people of Belsen for six months' treatment in Swedish sanatoria. On June 19th the first Red Cross train left Bergen-Belsen for Lübeck with three hundred and fifty lying cases and fifty sitting cases on board. Only after this first train had left was it realised that many of these sick people had healthy relatives in Belsen, who had avoided separation from them in the concentration camps, and who had cared for them and helped them. Were these families to be torn apart now after liberation?

In line with the official policy of British Military Government it was decided that efforts must be made to send healthy, 'first grade' relatives to Sweden with the sick. By 'first grade' relatives was meant mothers, fathers, children, brothers or sisters. But such a policy was easier to lay down than to carry through.

There was first of all the physical difficulty of discovering which of the sick people had healthy relatives in Belsen, and then that of finding these relatives. Each afternoon, during the evacuation, Sgt. C. and Sgt. H. used to walk through the hospital wards asking patients, who would leave for Sweden

next day, for the locations of any relatives they had in the camp. The difficulty was with convalescent cases, the 'sitting cases'. They were so far recovered that they were often strolling in the woods or fields when the sergeants visited their ward to question them. And many of the healthy relatives were equally elusive the following morning when it was time to start.
[. . .]
But the difficulty of locating and contacting the relatives of the sick was infinitesimal compared with the task of sifting non-genuine from genuine 'first grade' relations. For it must be remembered that the people of Belsen had no identity documents except what the British had issued, and for the personal histories of the thousands of inmates we had to rely upon the accounts they themselves gave.

Derrick Sington[7]

Han was besieged in her little office by a mob of relations who wanted to go to Sweden. It had become known that the Swedes had made a general offer to take all the sick from Belsen into their country. They said that their general policy would be to 'keep families together'. Hence, if a sick child was being taken the mother could go as well and any other well children in the same family. If both parents were dead and if an aunt was actually acting as mother, she would be permitted to go, but uncles and other relatives could not be considered. This ruling resulted in the creation of thousands of aunts, genuine and imaginary, who came claiming the most profound affection for every orphan child we had. They protested in Polish; they wept in Hungarian; they howled in Roumanian and all spoke together in a sort of German.

Robert Collis and Han Hogerzeil[8]

[Letter written in August 1945]

Dear Lady Oliver, [. . .]
When the No. 9 General Hospital moved to Hamburg Dr Collis [of the Red Cross] asked me to take over the Orphan Children's Home. I started with over 100 children consisting of eleven nationalities and ages ranging between 20 months and 16 years.
Most of the children could speak German and 54 of them slept in a huge attic, boys and girls mixed. It was astonishing how they all looked after themselves and helped each other to keep clean.
In the early days meals rather resembled feeding time at the Kennels, but food was still a novelty and I turned many a blind eye to what could well be described as hideous table manners, but as the excitement of every meal waned so did the wild rush and scramble to eat. By the time we left Belsen for Sweden we were nearly civilised.

Many children were repatriated during June and July, and on Monday 23 July I left Belsen for Sweden with 51 Orphan children and two grown up Displaced Persons together with Dr Collis, Sister [Cruas?] and two Dutch girls attached [to the Red Cross] and some 66 sick children, various others and other attachments including illegitimate Norwegian /German babies.

We started loading the hospital train at Belsen at 1pm and we left at 6pm and travelled all night. We arrived at Lubeck next morning and remained in the Swedish Transit Hospital in the Barracks area until 11am the following day.

We all had to be scrubbed and bathed by the Swedish Red Cross, who are nothing if not thorough. The fact that there was very little privacy seemed a minor detail in the eyes of the Swedes and one of the Dutch girls found herself sharing the hot steam bath tent with several Swedish women and also a member of the other sex. I had just left the tent before the arrival of the latter!

We boarded the Swedish Red Cross Ship SS Kastelholm on Wednesday at about 11am and arrived at Malmö in Sweden on Thursday afternoon. We were all very cramped on board and most of 'my' children were below deck in cabins with no port holes, and they suffered a good deal from a rather suffocating heat and had headaches and felt sick.

It was all rather exhausting and on arrival in Malmö the children were all fed in a huge shed on the Quay but the BRC personnel got nothing. We were then divided up into groups and sent off for more scrubbing and baths and medical inspections. This went on until midnight by which time several of the children were crying from fatigue and others had hysterical giggles. We were then put into a huge bus and taken on a two hours run to a place a few miles from Helsingborg-Sundsgarden.

The driver lost his way several times and the exhausted children were lying asleep all over the bus.

We received a warm and friendly welcome from the Swedish Sisters at Sundsgarden (a school during term time) and after everyone had been sorted out and carried off to bed. I was taken to a wee room on the top floor and found one of the Dutch girls already asleep in the second bed. Her group had arrived some four hours earlier.

We got up at 7am with the rest of the staff and were very shaken to discover that breakfast was not until 10am.

Twenty two hours without food after several days of strenuous travelling was rather like the camel's last straw, but we helped to cut the bread for the children and to adjust ourselves to very strange surroundings. There was a large staff of Swedish sisters and only one could speak English, none could speak French and only two knew a few words of German.

The Belsen mothers and children were very Belsen-Homesick. They found the rather severe manners of the Swedes very different to the British Tommies' easy humour and to the freedom allowed them by the BRCS and I had hard work to explain that the Swedes were really being very kind, and also trying to give the Swedes a clear picture of the horrors the women and children had been through.

I think my liaison efforts were successful as everyone seemed more settled when I left on 1st August.

Enid Fernandes, *British Red Cross*[9]

Evacuation of patients has been carried out at a rapid pace. Hospital train after train has left, packed with mostly lying patients, many accompanied by relatives, for the policy is to keep families together as much as possible. I went to see a train depart for Sweden the other evening and the OC took me right through. There were 320 patients, many of them thin, ill and unhappy-looking, others brighter and more cheerful. It was 6pm and they were having their tea, which consisted of dark rye bread and butter and a tin of peculiar, greyish-looking fish floating in a more peculiar murky-looking liquid, which they appeared to relish. Some of the patients looked very ill – the doctor did not expect one girl to reach her destination, but wanted to give her the satisfaction of leaving Belsen.

[. . .]

I love to visit the camp squares on the occasions when a transport is leaving with happy, well-fed, warmly clad repatriates. Army trucks and lorries which convey them are stocked with food and decorated with garlands, branches and national flags. Sometimes a band plays as they are being comfortably seated with their worldly possessions around them, and the Military Government and voluntary organisation officials farewell them. With the singing of National Anthems and much hand waving they leave us to start life once again in their own country as the long convoy passes out of sight.

Muriel Knox Doherty, *Chief Nurse and Principal Matron,*
United Nations Relief and Rehabilitation Administration,
from letter dated 25th August 1945[10]

LIST OF TITLES AND FUNCTION OF THE MEMBERS OF THE CENTRAL JEWISH COMMITTEE, BERGEN-BELSEN CONCENTRATION CAMP

THE PRAESIDIUM comprising the Chairman, Yossel Rosensaft, Dr Hadassah Bimko and Berl Loifer. As the official representatives of the Committee they were to oversee the work of the departments and assume responsibility for all contacts with the 'outside world.'

THE SECRETARIAT   which would undertake the registration of all arrivals at the camp, compile accurate statistics indicating the numbers who wished to return to their country of origin, and the numbers of children in various camps of given ages.

A RECORD ROOM   in which the 98 centres in which Jews were to be found were to be listed and from which circulars, prepared for distribution, would be issued.

INFORMATION   to assist in the search for relatives who may be found in the various centres in the British and American zones. To this end a card index of survivors was to be compiled in the hope of ultimately publishing a comprehensive list of all DPs.

STORES   from which clothing and amenities would be distributed to selected cases, especially to the children and the sick in hospitals.

CULTURE   The presence in the camp of Chaim Feder, a well-known Yiddish artiste, led to the formation of a theatrical group which presented plays and recitals in the camp. This department also encouraged inmates to write diaries and compose poems and songs which would reflect the life and experiences of the inmates.

EDUCATION   In spite of the shortage of text books, courses were to be organised on such subjects as Hebrew, English, mathematics and art. Special attention to be given to the school opened in collaboration with the Jewish Relief Team.

PRESS   Attempts were made to produce a camp newspaper entitled *Unsere Shtimme* [Our Voice]. [...]

HEALTH   Each block in the camp to be scrupulously watched to ensure its hygienic condition was maintained. The hospitals to be regularly visited and amenities distributed to the patients.

CHILDREN AND YOUTH   In addition to the children's home, established to house some 30 orphan children between the ages of 10 to 14, every encouragement was to be given to the various Zionist movements, both religious and secular, which developed in the camp.

Reverend Isaac Levy[11]

REPORT ON 'JEWISH CONGRESS' AT HÖHNE CAMP
25–27 SEPTEMBER [1945]. BY MAJOR C. C. K. RICKFORD,
POLICY SEC. PWDP DIV. CONTROL COMMISSION

[...]
The organisation and direction of the Congress was excellent. All factions were accorded a hearing at the insistence of the Chairman, including communists and those advocating a return to their previous countries. Both these latter views were extremely unpopular with the large majority.
[...]

The purpose of the meeting appears to have been to contact Jewish DPs all over Germany and to endeavour to band them together. To influence them to bring up their children as Jews and to secure a revival of enthusiasm for the Jewish faith and national spirit. It became obvious very early on that a claim to return to Palestine was the main objective, and as a corollary the demand for segregation now into Jewish Camps in order to train the community for its future life in Palestine.

The conference was conducted in German and Yiddish, with a few speeches in English and Hungarian. A great deal of repetition and rhetoric was in evidence.

Despite a few enthusiastic anti-Zionists the meeting was overwhelmingly in favour of the opening of Palestine to such as wished to go there, and of immediate segregation into Jewish Camps.

General Points from speeches:
Historical: A great deal of time was devoted to a historical survey of the persecution of Jews in Europe
Religious: A number of appeals were made by Rabbis and others for a return to the orthodox faith.
Zionism: A good many speakers devoted their addresses to proof of the claim of the Jews to Palestine and toward pictures of the promised land.
Complaints: A few complaints were made about present conditions, notably the following:
  – Robbing of DPs by British Guards
  – Unauthorised search and removal of cigarettes and food from DPs entering the camp
  – Complaints against the food, particularly lack of bulk (bread), and green vegetables (Mr Brodetsky has taken a specimen day's ration to the UK)
  – Overcrowding viz. two in a bed
  – Staffing of the hospital with Germans
  – General feeling of being regarded as 'second-rate' human beings
Claims made for the Community
  – Freedom of speech and discussion
  – Right to publish a Jewish newspaper
  – Removal of guards and wire
  – Right of equality as human beings
  – Right to determine their own destiny in their own way in their own country – Palestine
[...]
Military Security:
It was thought that a certain number of people might have succeeded in entering the British Zone without permission, in order to attend the

conference. So far as was ascertainable only [a few?] DPs have arrived from outside the Zone, including some from Poland, and from Czechoslovakia. A few persons from the Lüneburg Trial also attended.

Conclusion:
Pending a statement of policy on the Palestine question, it is quite certain that a good deal of agitation may be expected regarding the conditions and treatment of Jewish DPs.
[...]
Appendix B – Resolutions of Jewish Congress held at Hohne 25–27 Sep 45 (Translation from the original Yiddish as telegraphed to London for the Press)

1.a) The first Congress of the Remnants of Israel in Germany liberated from concentration camps through the victories of the United Nations, profoundly conscious of its historical responsibility for the fate of the forty thousand Jews it represents, wholeheartedly endorses the resolutions adopted at the World Zionist Conference in London, and at the Conference of the World Jewish Congress, and asks the British Government and Allied Nations:
   – To designate Palestine as a Jewish State
   – To vest the Jewish agency with the control of immigration into Palestine and with the necessary authority to develop the resources of the country.
   – To effect the transfer of the first million Jews to Palestine and to raise an international loan for this purpose
   – To ensure that the countries of Jewish emigration facilitate this transfer in every way.

b) In the name of 6,000,000 Jews who have fallen victims of the German terror, and in the name of the survivors, we call on the peoples of the world, and particularly on the British Nation, which carries a special responsibility in this respect, to recognise that the world will know no peace as long as the Jewish people is denied the right which exists for other people to determine its destiny in its own land. We call on the world to realise that the extermination of 6,000,000 Jews in Auschwitz, Trehlinda [Treblinka], Naidanck [Majdanek], Belsen and other centres was possible only because of the homelessness and statelessness of the Jewish people.

c) We demand the right to guard our children and the coming generations against a repetition of this disaster.

d) We appeal to the United Nations and to England in particular, to end the homelessness of the Jewish people. We affirm our right of immigration into Palestine, sealed with the blood of millions, and demand its immediate realisation.

e) We, representatives of the remnant assembled here in Bergen-Belsen, express our sorrow and indignation that almost six months after liberation we still find ourselves in guarded camps on German soil soaked with the blood of our people.

f) We proclaim that we will not be driven back into the lands which have become the mass graveyards of our people.

g) We vow that no obstacle or political restriction will bar our way to Palestine and warn those concerned of the consequences which will flow from a policy in conflict with the vital interests of the Jewish people.

2.a) This congress demands that as long as Jewish survivors remain in Germany they shall be recognised as Jews and not as nationals of countries to which they do not intend to return.

b) This congress urges that opportunities be created for training the survivors for productive life in Palestine; that Jewish Camps and centres be established both in British and American Zones, under Jewish Administration, and that Jewish liaison officers be appointed with the Mil. Gov. in Germany.

c) This congress asks that the property of destroyed Jewish communities, and of individual Jews who perished without successors shall be placed at the disposal of the representative body of the Jewish people for the purpose of further development of Palestine.

d) The congress asks a special allocation be made from German reparations for life pensions for all Jews disabled and rendered invalid in German concentration camps.

e) This congress requests Jewish Representation at the International Commission for War Crimes.

f) This congress asks for the recognition of the Central Jewish Committee as the legal representative body of all former inmates of German Concentration Camps in the British and American Zones.

g) This congress states that five months after liberation it is still impossible for them to correspond with their relatives and demands an immediate change in this abnormal position.

h) This congress greets the Jewish Brigade to which it feels itself united by ties of brotherhood and common struggle.

3. This congress finally resolves that a memorandum setting forth the conditions and needs of the Jews in Germany shall be submitted together with the resolutions of this congress to Generals Montgomery and Eisenhower.

Major C. C. K. Rickford, *Policy Section, PW & DP Division*[12]

On Tuesday last, 25th September [1945], I was invited to Camp 1 to the unveiling of a Jewish memorial to the thousands of Jews who are buried there and the hundreds of thousands more who perished elsewhere. I think it was the Day of Atonement. Thousands of Jewish survivors (and there are about 9,000 at present in this camp) and other DPs marched from the present camp carrying banners of blue and white with various mottoes. The granite memorial is erected near one of the immense graves holding thousands of nameless people who were either dead or died soon after liberation, before the British were able to evacuate them. We drove there and, standing on an elevated piece of ground, were able to watch the seemingly endless procession as it approached. So many had been in the Horror Camp, and many had lost all their people there, while others had come to pay tribute to their unfortunate fellows who knew no earthly liberation. While we were waiting for the ceremony to commence, I was introduced to Brigadier Glyn-Hughes, who did such famous work at Belsen. I asked him to point out the perimeter of the actual area in which the victims of Nazi brutality had been confined: $^4/_5$ x $^2/_5$ of a mile only, in which more than 50,000 living and unburied dead had been concentrated.

The ceremony was in Yiddish and the Rabbi, who spoke from one of the German observation posts, was evidently very melodramatic for he moved the multitude so that the sobbing came as the soft twittering of many birds in distant trees at dusk. It was terrible. I stood on the bonnet of our car and was able to look down on the crowd, mostly young men and women. You could pick out many of those who had been in the Horror Camp – their hair had grown fine and sparse, due to illness and starvation. [...]

Muriel Knox Doherty, *letter dated 27 September 1945*[13]

The library in Camp 3 was not used a great deal at first. Partly because of a rule that books must not be taken away, but partly also because a craving for pleasure rather than for knowledge possessed a great part of the survivors. This was true particularly of the young women. After the years of repression, gloom, terror and want their pent-up desire to live could at last be satisfied. They wanted to 'live' rather than to think. This did not apply to all inmates of Camp 3, for four hundred people registered their names for English classes in three days, and usually in the library there were three or four people browsing over books or newspapers. The women read mostly novels and love stories. The true 'intellectual' was rare, though I remember one young man who was embarking on a German translation of the Brothers Karamazov.

We soon realised that to the mass of the people in Belsen entertainment and sport would make a greater appeal than books. Eva Stojowska, a Polish actress, with ten years' experience at the Warsaw National Theatre, suggested the production of an international cabaret. The two Red Cross ladies and I called on each of the national committees and asked them to try to mobilise theatrical talent for a show to be given during the following week.

On May 24th this 'International Cabaret' was given in the dining-hall of Canteen 2 in Camp 3. It included some Polish dances, a charming choir of tiny Russian girls singing partisan songs and children's songs, a choir of Yugoslav partisan women, tough and amazonian in blue slacks and white pullovers, and songs from operas sung by Eva Stojowska. A vivacious but rather gaunt Hungarian woman played Czardas music on her violin with immense tempo. She had just recovered from typhus. Her name was Lili Mathé and she had once played outside the great crematoria at Auschwitz, by order of Josef Kramer, while the truck-loads of doomed men and women rolled into the camp.

For the second of these international entertainments we decided to use the tented theatre of the Panzer Training School. This was a gigantic tent erected on aluminium struts. It seated eight hundred people and had an excellently equipped stage complete with foot-lights, spot-lights and wings. The dressing-rooms were built in the form of railway coaches and were stamped 'Strength Through Joy'. For this unusual theatre had been constructed on the orders of Dr. Ley, as a mobile unit, to be transported bodily to isolated village-communities which had no facilities for dramatic shows. It had been manufactured in Friedrichshaven in the Zeppelin factory, and indeed the inside of it resembled that of a gigantic airship. Early in the war it had been handed over to the Wehrmacht and established at the Panzer Training School for the entertainment of the German troops.

Derrick Sington[14]

Belsen Camp, 30th July 1945

My dearest H[elli]

... On Friday Yehudi Menuhin was here in Belsen Camp. At first it seemed as if this concert was going to be 'for Poles only', and we were really furious, but it then transpired that it was not meant literally and we got tickets without any trouble.

It was a wonderful evening. Both soloist and accompanist were dressed in simple attire bordering on the slovenly, which matched the surroundings perfectly. It goes without saying that Menuhin played faultlessly; he is after all Yehudi Menuhin. But I must confess (and please don't take this as impertinence on my part) that I was a little disappointed. His playing didn't have the soul that I imagine Casals has. I had the distinct impression that he was saving himself. It could well be that he did not find the atmosphere very inspiring. For it was impossible to get complete silence in the hall, and I was thoroughly ashamed of the audience. In fact it was amazing that he did not just stop in midstream.

As for his accompanist, I can only say that I cannot imagine anything done more beautifully. He was completely unobtrusive and yet I found myself transfixed by him sitting there as if he wouldn't say boo to a goose – but playing to perfection. (The accompanist was none other than Benjamin Britten, it emerged later.)

Yes, who would ever have believed that Belsen Camp would hear Yehudi Menuhin playing? By the way, he played the Bach/Kreisler Prelude and Fugue, the *Kreutzer Sonata*, Mendelssohn's Concerto, something by Debussy and several smaller, unfamiliar items.

Anita Lasker-Wallfisch, *survivor of Auschwitz and Belsen*[15]

I had occasion to take a Polish Priest, Fr. Kiek, to the distant village one day in July. He was one of the younger priests to survive and was now energetic in his ministry for the community of Poles still in the camp. One of the huts had been converted into a Chapel for their own use. A London-born Italian working with the British Red Cross fell in love with an attractive Polish girl. They consulted Fr. Kiek and asked him to publish their banns of marriage. It fell on my shoulders to establish the man's freedom to marry, while Fr. Kiek was faced with the problem of proving hers, because as soon as the banns were published some Jewesses objected to the marriage, maintaining that the girl had been employed in the officers mess and was already married to an SS officer. It was clearly impossible to get any documentary evidence of this, therefore Fr. Kiek had to find somebody who knew the girl and her family well enough to testify by affidavit on her behalf. He discovered that two or three such people were among those who had recently been evacuated to the village fifty odd miles away. I took him there by car and he eventually found them and they were only too glad to help. The girl came of a very respectable family, and by working in the officers quarters she probably saved her life. The SS had already murdered her parents, uncles and aunts and closer relations. It was unthinkable that she would ever want to marry such a brutalised character. The Chapel was beautifully decorated and the happy bride and groom duly married. News of the event had already spread beyond the camp. The 'Daily Mail' sent a photographer and prided itself on publishing a photograph of the first wedding to be celebrated in Belsen camp.

Reverend Father Edmund Swift, S. J., *R. C. Chaplain to 81 British General Hospital*[16]

I was a guest at a DP's wedding on 21st July. A Polish girl from Camp 1 who had been very ill with typhus had met an ambulance driver of the BRCS who had worked at the evacuation of the Horror Camp. Her name was Toni Sucheka and the groom's Pitrucchi, British, of Italian parentage. In full bridal attire, she looked very attractive. The ceremony was held in the Roman

Catholic 'church', a room in one of the blocks, which was decorated with scarlet rowan-berries, blue lupins and white flowers. A red carpet runner with bunches of oak leaves placed at intervals on either side was appropriate. Potted shrubs from the Round House added to the decorations.

The service was short and a Polish DP sang 'Ave Maria' to the accompaniment of a croaky harmonium. The bride's veil had little sprigs of green leaves attached, with a half coronet of the same round the back of her head. I do not know whether this is a national custom or not. She carried a bouquet of a white flower which is plentiful here at present – a cross between white lilac and hydrangea, but I do not know its name. The civil ceremony was combined with the signing of the register. A Polish reception was held first among her friends and then the BRCS gave one in their tented mess. There were Hungarian and Polish cakes and biscuits, sandwiches, and two wedding cakes. The Red Cross in Brussels sent a bottle of champagne and Dr Collis, BRCS, made a speech. There was a box full of presents of all varieties. Streamers of surgical gauze decorated the car in bridal fashion. The happy pair went away for their honeymoon to Copenhagen, I think. You may probably have seen photos of this wedding, which figured in all the British papers.

Muriel Knox Doherty, *letter dated August 1945*[17]

On Tuesday I had a special invitation to the first Belsen wedding, a Lithuanian girl and Polish man, both Jews. The ceremony was most peculiar and took place in the hall under a gold and red canopy held up by four ruffians. The bride was very charming but the man a real tough. After the wedding the guests, about 100, sat down to a real feast, officers, ranks, British Red Cross Society and all the nationalities of Europe. I was very amused to find my opposite had a reticule under the table in which she deposited everything she could lay hands on, including the cutlery! This of course is typical of Belsen, nothing is private property! After supper we had dancing complete with Military Band. I was a bit worn out by dancing three times running with the Jewish Rabbi, who said it was the first time he had danced in five years and it certainly felt like it. I was pleased to have on army shoes!

Miss Margaret Wyndham Ward, *British Red Cross Society,*
letter of 23 June 1945[18]

MY TIME WITH THE JEWISH RELIEF UNIT

Some time in 1943 the 'Council of British Societies for Relief Abroad' was founded in view of the sad events on the Continent. The Anglo-Jewish Community felt the need to represent their group and formed the 'Jewish Committee for Relief Abroad' under the auspices of the Central British Fund.

They hoped to organise Jewish teams to help suffering of liberated survivors, if possible. [...] In the summer of 1943 a Training Camp was held at Tring Park not far from London, the property belonging to Lord Rothschild, and made available. We were 68 people, 49 men and 19 women, coming from all walks of life, many from London, a number from Manchester. One of those was Mr Leonard Cohen, one of the first volunteers, who was the Director. Many others had been social workers in London or elsewhere.

But it was only after the end of the War, that the first team was allowed to leave for the Continent. I myself had been fortunate to come to Britain [from Germany] in November 1938 as a nursing student. I became a registered nurse in 1942 working in hospitals. By summer 1945 I was 1) 'Enemy Alien' and 2) in a 'reserved occupation' so was not able to leave anywhere before September 1946, when 3 of us were given permission to depart for Europe. We were given Army uniforms and supplies. [...] In the British Zone the largest concentration of Survivors outside some of the larger cities were found in the Bergen-Belsen Camp; that's where we were taken about 1 week later – which happened to be shortly before Rosh Hashonah.

After a bit of getting to know people and locations I started to work with the children; some of them were orphans and were taken care of in a Children's Home, others living with a parent or relative. By this time, some of the surviving younger people had gotten married and we tried to teach these young women the basics of hygiene, basic nutrition and healthy living habits.

One of the other team members was Eva (Minden) Kahn who had arrived a little before me. She was a Nurse-Midwife and mainly worked at the Glyn-Hughes Hospital, which was mainly staffed by German doctors and nurses. She made sure the Jewish patients were properly taken care of. Many times she and I made decisions together in looking after the people. She also eventually started to give basic nursing instructions to a group of about 10 or 12 young women, giving them fundamental lectures on First Aid and similar subjects. After she had left to go back to England, I took her place, dealing with matters in the hospital and some teaching.

The winter of 1946–47 was a very harsh one, and by that time the word had gotten around about this large community of Jewish survivors in Belsen, and so we found a large influx of people coming into the Camp from the East. Our team as a group in our various jobs tried to accommodate the new arrivals. The Camp Committee made up of survivors themselves had become sort of a community in itself, with their rules and regulations.

Our JRU team-leader was Sarah (Eckstein) Grebenau [...] One of our team members was a teacher at the school in Belsen; there had been a few doctors as well; several were social workers. We worked together, trying to cover needs as they arose, many times together with the Joint [American Joint

Distribution Committee] members when locating missing relatives. Overall, I think that we from the 'Jewish Relief' learned a great deal in human nature in those days. We tried to be of some help under the conditions at that time to the best of our ability.

Alice Fink, *Jewish Relief Unit*[19]

By the time I arrived at Bergen-Belsen which was several weeks after its liberation, the Jewish community and its leadership had begun to have some sense of an organisation. They had already identified 83 children under the age of 16 who had absolutely no relatives. It's amazing, when you think if it: there were 10,000 persons in Bergen-Belsen and there were only 83 surviving orphan children – a handful. Since I was the Child Welfare Officer, I was put in charge of them. We located a building and decided to house all those children together, in what became know as the 'Kinderheim' – The House of the Children.

The first day that the children were in their house, we issued sheets and blankets. The next morning, I was told that nobody had any blankets. And I said – 'How come?'. And shamefacedly, the woman in charge [...] said – 'They sold it to the Germans for better stuff.' And it was that day that I realised that there was an awful lot that I did not know about the Bergen-Belsen children. I called them all together and I made my first great speech – I said 'Ok, you got rid of your blankets last night, I'm not going to make any judgement about that, I'll try to get 83 more blankets, but that is it. The next time you get rid of the blankets you can freeze for the rest of the time you are in Bergen-Belsen.' I think most of the kids got the message but the few that sold them again fortunately found other ways to stay warm. I'm sad to say that many weeks later when Larry my fiancée came to visit me at Bergen-Belsen, no sooner had he left his jeep unattended, his camera was taken. I had the feeling that, if the children had known that in some way he belonged to me, perhaps they would have resisted this robbery, but I'm not sure about that.

[...]

Bergen-Belsen children – the children of the Children's House – began to settle into some kind of normal life. They began to fight with each other, they had puppy-love romances, there was plenty of acting out, they objected to the rules, and night after night, more than one of those children cried themselves to sleep. One day when we were working in the Children's House there was a terrific shout, and I went out to see what was going on. And in the yard was Pola and Bella's father. In all the time that I was in Europe, and certainly in Bergen-Belsen, that was the only intact family I ever knew: the mother was in hospital, and now, their father had arrived from Poland. It was the best of days, and the worst of days. Can you imagine what it was like for the other children whose families had perished?

As life moved forward in Bergen-Belsen, we established some kind of order for the kids. They were restless; it was clear that there was going to be no quick rescue for anybody languishing in the DP camps. All the Displaced Persons believed that since they were a handful and were liberated, the rest of the world was going to come and get them, and coming to get them immediately. But there was no way that that was going to happen. Clearly they were going to have to have a long, long stay in the Camp. So we began to have a life. [. . .]

As life moved forward, the whole Bergen-Belsen community began to organise itself and developed a magnificent theatre group. Not really hard for them because about ten of the people in the camp had been actors and actresses in the famous Habima theatre in Poland. There were regular performances put on in Bergen-Belsen. They decided, as they got better and better, to do a performance for the British Military. I was asked if I would be the MC. They decided that my English was rather good as was my Yiddish and that I would make an excellent MC. The children said 'Well, if you're going to be the MC and you belong to us, then you have to get us seats!' And I said, 'Sorry, this is a show for the military, this is not for you; you cannot go' – 'But this is going to be the best show – the big show!' – 'Sorry, you cannot go.' The evening of the show, I go out on stage and say in Yiddish and in English 'Good evening', and before I say more than that, there's a terrific cheering and clapping and I looked down and every single child of the Children's House in Bergen-Belsen is in the front row!

[. . .]

A talented woman, Sala Lewkowicz, who had been a principal at a school in Warsaw, organised a school in Bergen-Belsen for our children. And that was a new problem. Now we had to get children up to go to school, who hadn't been to school for five years – but they went.

And then somewhere after the time we had been in Bergen for about six months, we suddenly noticed that there were new and different soldiers in the camp. And very soon we understood that they were from the Palestinian Brigade, the Jewish Brigade. The war was over, they had not yet been sent back to Israel, which was then Palestine, and so they moved illegally to Bergen-Belsen. Some of them were teachers so they worked in the schools. Others worked in the camp. Soon their real mission became apparent. Our five vehicles were comfortably parked in the large yard adjoining Kolman's [the guest house outside Belsen where she and other JRU workers were staying]. One evening, the leader of the Palestinian Brigade named Vishnyak came to see us: 'There's only one reason why we are here: we are going to start to move people out of Bergen-Belsen to Marseilles and across the Mediterranean to Palestine illegally, and we would like you to help us, and we need your vehicles.' I said, 'Sorry, we can't do that, because we are only here by the courtesy of the British Government; we encourage you, but we can't help.' And I remember Vishnyak looking at me and saying: 'We are going to do this. You can't stop us: your choice is to help or keep silent.' And from that point on, from Kolman's, they moved people out of Bergen-Belsen, beginning them on their illegal journey. Many of the people that were on the Exodus came out of Bergen-Belsen. And after we really got into this and saw how it worked, the women on the Unit were asked if we would accompany the trucks, and we said 'Yes, we would, but why?' And they said: 'You speak better English than the Palestinians, and particularly as women you will be useful.' So we worked all day, and many a night we took illegal immigrants as far as the Dutch border, and fortunately we were never stopped. One of the things that I said to Vishnyak when he roped us in to this operation was: 'You're not going to take the children are you?' And he said 'No, we're not going to take the children: it's too dangerous, too tough a trip for them.'

I went back to the Children's Home, and wondered: "What is going to happen to our children?" They were going to makeshift schools; they certainly had food and plenty to eat; they needed far better medical care than we could give them in Bergen-Belsen. The British Government and the Jewish community in England were beginning to work to bring the children out. They knew that there were these 80–90 children in Bergen-Belsen – orphans. One day we received a message from the British Government: 'Please ready the children; we are going to take them to England; by next Saturday they should be at the airport; we are going to send planes for them.'

The Jewish leader of Bergen-Belsen – a wonderful man named Josef Rosensaft – was adamant: 'Those children are not going to leave Bergen-Belsen.' I said: 'Josef, we have to let them go. The British would take good care of them.' You may remember that in those days, one couldn't just go to Israel freely: Israel wasn't even Israel until 1948. If you wanted to emigrate from Britain to Palestine there was a quota: and they only allowed so many people to go at a time. The British promised however that these children would be the first allowed to go on a quota to Palestine. Josef said: 'Sadie, these are not *your* children, these are *our* children, and they are just a handful.' I argued: 'You cannot use them as a political football, you have to let them go.' Josef replied: 'Sadie, if we let the children go out of Bergen-Belsen, we will be here for years longer. As long as they are writing stories in London and New York about children in Bergen-Belsen, we have a chance to get out.' Days and days we argued; the planes were due the following day. But Josef remained firm.

I went to sleep that night and I didn't know what was going to happen. I knew that the planes were arriving at Celle airport the next day, and I thought – 'Well, whatever will be, will be.' About six o'clock in the morning, the telephone rang, and Major Murphy – the Camp Commander – invited me to his office. When I arrived, he was not alone. His guest spoke first. 'What is your name?' – 'My name is Sadie Rurka' – 'How old are you, Sadie Rurka?' – 'I'm twenty-two'. 'Well,' he said 'Sadie Rurka, you're a little too young for the problems of the Jewish people to be sitting on your shoulders, so I came.' I then realised he was David Ben-Gurion – indeed a more appropriate negotiator! The children did go to England.

Sadie Hofstein (née Rurka), *Jewish Relief Unit*[20]

FAREWELL TO BELSEN

I visited Belsen for the last time, recently. The Jewish DPs are fast leaving it. With large transports departing every month for Israel, it will soon be no more than a byword and a memory to world Jewry. Two years ago, when I first saw the camp, it was a thriving barrack town of some 12,000 Jews, frustrating, bleak, but alive.

The life of the camp was an experience which neither its adult residents nor the relief workers and regular visitors will forget. For the orphan children there it was accepted as normality in abnormality.

These orphan children lived in a long, low building of white stone, and at one time the sixty of them, aged from five to fourteen, were so crowded that they slept two to a narrow bed. Organised into groups by responsible young *madrichim*, they were kept busy and happy, and one rarely saw a tearful eye.

Boys and girls slept in separate rooms with others of their group, and lived like brothers and sisters, sharing the household chores. Yet the stagnation of the camp, through which they passed daily on their way to and from the school, could not be kept from them and the task of teaching them normal ways was not easy.

Their background was varied, as they had come from every type of home in every East European country, and Poles, Hungarians, and the rest were equally fond of the *Kinderheim* mascot, a jolly little Jewish boy from China. They spoke a dozen languages, but while Yiddish was known by most, Hebrew was taught to and understood by all. Hebrew was also the teaching language in the school, as otherwise a new Tower of Babel would have resulted.

'SHPIELST DU PING-PONG?'

My first time in the *Kinderheim* I could speak no Yiddish and only through halting Hebrew and the copious use of gesture could I make myself understood. Yet their insistent demands of '*Ess! Ess!*' as they piled black bread and herring on my plate at table allowed of no misunderstanding. After the meal they sang, and I was able to join in the same 'shirim' as are sung by Zionist youth groups in England. When finally a lad said to me, 'Gavriel, shpielst du ping-pong?' I was delighted to be able to understand him, consented, was led to the local sports club – and soundly beaten. It was a short step from this to promising to attempt revenge, visiting them often, and getting to know them and their needs and problems.

[...]

OLDER THAN THEIR YEARS

All the children had one thing in common – they were far older than their years. A child of six would talk politics with you rather than games. When they became friendly, they would tell you stories almost too horrible to be believed. Yossele, aged eight, speaks seven languages. He related in a matter-of-fact manner how his family fled from Poland, living short periods in Russia, Turkestan, and Afghanistan; how his parents were killed, and how at the end of the war he and his sister 'went down the American Zone.' 'Alone?' I asked him. 'Avada! Certainly alone,' he answered with dignity.

[...]

However normal these children may appear on the surface, their experiences have had certain general effects on them. They have had to fend for themselves for so long that they are usually either highly self-confident or else over-shy and reserved. Their minds, lacking schooling, are sharpened by experience, and to their teachers they appear unusually intelligent. Given the chance, they love to play, and the lads in the Belsen *Kinderheim* went wild with excitement when presented with a football. Give the girls dolls and they find new happiness.

What stood out most, however, with the children was their desperate need for affection. A group leader had to try to fulfil the functions of mother, father, nurse and teacher to about ten children. Home life gone, group loyalty was extreme, and an attempt to break up one little *kibbutz* while on convalescent holiday in Switzerland was unsuccessful, and the children were eventually housed together again.

Greville Janner, *article in the* Jewish Chronicle[21]

NOTES

1. The camp was established by the Nazis in 1943. The DP camp was shut in 1950 but the last Displaced Persons left the site of the post-liberation hospital area in 1952.
2. British Red Cross Archives, OFC1 drawer 3.
3. Anita Lasker-Wallfisch, *Inherit the Truth 1939–1945* (London: Giles de la Mare, 1996), p. 107.
4. From Isaac Levy, *Witness to Evil – Bergen-Belsen 1945* (London: Halban, 1995), p. 38–9.
5. IWM DD, 91/21/1.
6. *Belsen Uncovered* (London: Duckworth, 1946), pp. 205–6.
7. Ibid., pp. 193–4.

8. Robert Collis and Han Hogerzeil, *Straight On* (London: Methuen & Co. Ltd, 1947), pp. 92–3.

9. British Red Cross Archives, Acc X/104.

10. Muriel Knox Doherty, *Letters from Belsen 1945* (Crows Nest, NSW: Allen & Unwin, 2000), pp. 99–100.

11. Isaac Levy, *Witness to Evil – Bergen-Belsen 1945* (London: Halban, 1995), pp. 46–7.

12. Public Records Office Foreign Office 371/51125.

13. Muriel Knox Doherty, *Letters from Belsen 1945* (Australia: Allen & Unwin, 2000), pp. 141–2.

14. *Belsen Uncovered* (London: Duckworth, 1946), pp. 161–2.

15. Anita Lasker-Wallfisch, *Inherit the Truth 1939–1945*, p. 120.

16. IWM DD 90/4/1.

17. Muriel Knox Doherty, *Letters from Belsen 1945* (Crows Nest, NSW: Allen & Unwin, 2000), pp. 79–80.

18. British Red Cross Archives, AccX/278.

19. Account written by Alice Fink, held privately.

20. Expanded and amended text of talk given by Sadie Hofstein on 5 September 1995.

21. 8 April 1949.

Chapter 6
The Belsen Trial

The trial of the Belsen staff was the first of its kind in the British zone of occupation of Germany. It was conducted under the auspices of the Judge Advocate General's Department of the Army, pursuant to a piece of legislation known as the Royal Warrant. The trial began on 17 September 1945 in Lüneburg and lasted for two months. There were 45 defendants, chief among whom was the former camp commandant, Josef Kramer. The senior female defendant was the now infamous SS overseer Irma Grese. Many of the accused had also served at Auschwitz-Birkenau. Some were not SS personnel but rather inmate functionaries. The charges pertaining to Auschwitz mainly concerned 'selections' for the gas chambers. Those pertaining to Belsen – at which there were no gas chambers – concerned arbitrary executions and cruelties, the general harshness of the camp regime, and the starving of the inmates. Eleven of the defendants were sentenced to death, nineteen to prison terms varying from one year to life, and fifteen were acquitted.

Trials conducted under the Royal Warrant were tightly circumscribed in their legal scope, particularly when compared with the Nuremberg trial of the 'major war criminals' and its far-reaching legal basis as outlined in the London Charter of August 1945. The Royal Warrant permitted only prosecution of violations of 'the laws and customs of war' (thereby excluding consideration of the more broadly defined category of 'crimes against humanity'), and against nationals of Allied countries or countries occupied by Germany or its allies. Hence, in the first survivor testimony produced below, Harold Osmond Le Druillenec confronts the issue of trying – fruitlessly – to ascertain the national identity of particular murder victims in the camp. The effect of this focus was to exclude from official consideration crimes committed by, for instance, Germans against German Jews, and crimes committed in Germany before the outbreak of war.[1] It reflected a legal conservatism in the British Foreign and War Offices, and also the wider British wartime ambivalence, identified by the historian Tony Kushner,[2] about singling out Jewish suffering for particular attention in reactions to Nazi criminality.

Much of the trial revolved around the question of identification of individual guards or inmate functionaries and their association with specific acts of cruelty. This was not necessarily straightforward, as we shall see, since the prisoners did not always know the names of guards. Moreover, as Anita Lasker-Wallfisch observes, pinpointing a time and date upon which any given atrocity occurred among the multitude of atrocities was nigh impossible in a camp where one had neither watch nor calendar. Regina Bialek's evidence is an example of the type of detailed testimony needed by the prosecution for use against an individual defendant.

It is perhaps illustrative of British prejudices about the 'unreliability' of Jewish testimony that the first prosecution witnesses were drawn from the ranks of the military liberators. The first survivor witness, Le Druillenec, was not Jewish but was rather a Jersey schoolmaster, the only Briton known to have survived the camp.[3] The importance to the British of the question of nationality as opposed to ethno-religious identity ramified throughout the British trial programme in its official depiction of Jewish victims not as Jews as such, but rather as 'nationals' of given countries. (Thus in the trial of Zyklon B suppliers Bruno Tesch and two other members of his chemicals firm, the defendants were charged with providing 'poison gas used for the extermination of allied nationals [*sic*] in concentration camps'.)[4] Meanwhile, the press reporting, which peaked during the first month of the trial and dropped off rapidly thereafter, alternately accurately reported and misrepresented the specifically anti-Jewish thrust of the crimes being described in court, at one point identifying the Jews as the main victims, but at another neglecting to report who, specifically, was being sent to the Birkenau gas chambers. The Belsen trial, therefore, did not fully redress the de-Judaized depiction of the camps in the early press reporting of the camp and its liberation.[5]

The very idea of giving concentration camp guards and other perpetrators the benefit of due process was controversial to some, such as Lasker-Wallfisch. It is certainly the case that numerous defendants in various trials escaped with a lesser penalty than they deserved as a result of legal technicality. Conversely, trials such as the Belsen case certainly showed intent on the part of the Allies to assert the rule of law in international affairs. They also produced much useful documentary and eyewitness evidence on Nazi criminality. And although the Belsen trial, like all the British Royal Warrant cases, did not have the same scope as the American-led Nuremberg trial project, it can be seen as part of the same Allied attempt to address the crimes of Nazism, punish some of its main players, and re-educate Germany as a whole. The legacy of this broad Allied trial project was mixed.

We need to distinguish between the longer-term legal ramifications and the shorter-term political outcomes of the trial programme. In the short term, after the early determination in 1945–46 to purge Nazi Germany of its criminals, enthusiasm for trying Germans swiftly waned. By 1947, as the Cold War was beginning to descend, and the first moves were made towards rehabilitating West Germany as a bulwark against the USSR, for the Western Allies trials became undesirable politically. Legal proceedings were also a drain on financial resources, particularly for impoverished Britain. Both the British and the American trial programmes were further compromised in the early 1950s by the premature release of very large numbers of convicted war criminals to appease German nationalist sentiment and smooth the path for a German military contribution to western European defence.

In the longer term, the picture is brighter. The Nuremberg trial in particular firmly established the accountability under international law of leaders of state for acts of state. Some of the legal concepts devised and employed in that case were instrumental in shaping the 1948 Genocide Convention and current prosecutions of war crimes and crimes against humanity from Rwanda to The Hague.

*

At that time [in April 1945] it seemed unnecessary to put the camp guards on trial. Why not shoot them in front of the wretched people they've been torturing, and be done with it? Let it be known that there would be instant and drastic justice for anyone caught in such foul work as theirs.

But as the time has gone by, I've realised that a full-dress trial was right. Such crimes are too big and too grave to be expiated by a single shot of a firing squad. We must show in public the wickedness of such people and demonstrate that even in cases as extreme as this they are given a chance to prove themselves innocent. However much people may grumble at the time it takes and the money it costs, the fact remains that when the Lüneberg trial is over and the verdicts are given, the whole world will have been able to know – not in passion, but in cold proven legal detail – exactly what can happen behind the frontiers of a country that surrenders its soul to a dictator.

Meanwhile, we can take comfort from the fact that skill and, above all, humanity have made a wonderful job of the casualties of Belsen – right from that first day when Brigadier Glyn-Hughes went into camp alone. Now at Belsen there's a first-class hospital [. . .] While the Lüneburg trial condemns those who did the wrong, the Matron and her Sisters in the new Belsen are showing what kindness can do.

Richard Dimbleby, *BBC Pacific Service*[6]

It has been difficult to find any witnesses who had been in Belsen camp any length of time, and in the early days almost all the witnesses were rambling and incoherent. There was however a number of women brought from working camps near Bremen and Hamburg. These had had no food for seven days before liberation, but were able to give evidence. They knew little of

Belsen camp and the result is that the bulk of evidence recorded relates to crimes committed elsewhere. The higher officials of these camps moved from one camp to another so that there is in their stories evidence against Kramer, the commandant, and Klein, the doctor, captured at this camp.

[...]

The punishment of War Criminals after trial has been accepted as a war aim of the Allies. If this is to be carried out, reliable evidence must be collected and recorded. At the moment there is no organisation for doing this, probably because the volume of the evidence is unexpectedly great. [...] a wealth of evidence could be obtained, if a proper organisation was set up. It is most desirable that the officer collecting evidence at Belsen should know who is in custody at Sachsenhausen and vice versa. It is recommended that, if it has not already been done, a staff be set up to direct the collection of evidence and its collation.

Captain H. G. Sherrin, *Military Government Legal Officer,*
report dated 27 April 1945[7]

I, Harold Osmond Le Druillenec, at present at Horton Hospital, Epsom, Surrey, with permanent address at No 7 Trinity Road, St Helier, Jersey, schoolmaster, make oath and say as follows:

On 3 June 1944 I was arrested by the Germans at St Helier and taken to the Jacques Cartier Prison near Rheims, France [the prison was actually in Rennes]. I stayed there about a week when I was taken with other prisoners to Belfort. I stayed there about fourteen days. From there I was sent to Neuergamme [Nevengamme] Concentration Camp, arriving there about the beginning of September. I was next taken to Wilhelmshaven where I stayed until the 2nd April 1945. On that day I and several hundred other prisoners were sent to Belsen Concentration Camp, arriving there after a few days journey.

On arriving at Belsen we were offered some soup in exchange for either bread or cigarettes and only those prisoners who could give up some bread or cigarettes were able to obtain soup. We were taken to our blocks. I was in block 12. The whole camp was grossly overcrowded and at night six hundred of us were locked in a hut which might have accommodated one hundred. There was not sufficient room to lie down and we had to spend the night sitting up and jammed up against each other. At least eight or nine prisoners died each night. All the internees in my block were men, mostly Russians and Poles with some French and a mixture of other European races.

At 3.30am we had to get up and go on Appel – parade – where we had to stand to attention until 8am. We were then formed into parties of five and started dragging corpses to the burial pits. There were thousands of corpses lying in heaps almost all over the camp.

The German SS personnel – guards and others – were brutal to all prisoners. Every guard carried a stick or a piece of wood with which they continually beat internees on the head for no reason at all. I myself was beaten many times by the camp staff but I cannot say the names of any of the guards as I never knew their names.

Prisoners were shot out of hand indiscriminately, again for no reason at all, and all day shots could be heard all over the camp. Prisoners who were shot or beaten to death were left lying on the ground until some time later when their bodies were taken off to the burial pits.

During my first four days at Belsen I received in all not more than one pint of watery swede soup and one mug of water. During my last five days before the British troops entered the camp I had nothing to eat and nothing to drink.

Whilst dragging corpses to the burial pits I noticed that in many cases a piece of flesh had been cut off the body, generally from the back of the thigh and I was told that the flesh had been cut off and eaten. I myself saw on several occasions internees cutting flesh off corpses and stuffing it into their mouths, eating it like animals.

I cannot say the names or nationalities of any of the internees whom I saw killed or beaten as we did not know each others' names or nationality. I can only say that all the guards and officials habitually ill-treated all internees in this way.

I am of British nationality.

Harold Osmond Le Druillenec, *Deposition*[8]

(Further Deposition of Regina Bialek (female) late of Skladowa, 16, Lodz, Poland, sworn before Major Savile Geoffrey Champion, Royal Artillery, Legal Staff, No. 1 War Crimes Investigation Team)

Further to my deposition sworn on 26th May 1945:

I first met Helena Kopper when I travelled from Auschwitz to Belsen in the summer of 1944. During the time that we were in Belsen Camp Kopper told me that her husband and son were both members of the SS and that she came from Cracow. I first heard that her husband was a German from other prisoners and in order to find out the truth I told Kopper that my husband was a German. It was then that Kopper told me the story of her own husband and son. At Belsen Kopper acted as an assistant Block Ältester [elder/leader], and for a while as camp policeman. She was well favoured by the SS. Kopper reported to the SS the names of women who were in possession of valuables etc. and the SS then came to those women and deprived them of that property. Women found in possession of valuables were often beaten by the SS.

Kopper was assistant block Ältester of Block 27 in the women's camp at

Belsen and I was in this block whilst she was there. Kopper deprived women in the block of their proper share of what food there was because she kept more for herself than she was entitled to have. The food that she saved in this way she exchanged with other prisoners for margarine. Kopper frequently beat other women prisoners in the block for coming to her for more food. She beat them across the head and all parts of the body with a wooden stick, sometimes three or four times. As far as I know Kopper did not inflict any serious injuries on those she beat but there was no necessity for the beatings.

I have also seen Kopper beat women prisoners outside the block in the camp. As a camp policewoman she checked prisoners for small offences such as being outside the block when an alert was sounded. For these trifling offences she beat prisoners with a wooden stick and on one occasion she beat a friend of mine without reason. I did not see the incident but was told by my friend who had a black eye.

In Belsen Kopper used to keep company with one of the SS men. I do not know his name but he used to visit the block to see her and bring her packets of food. When he came other prisoners used to clear out the way. Kopper became pregnant according to other prisoners, and all said that the SS man was responsible. Then one day in March 1945 SS woman Ehlert came to the block to search for jewellery but she was unable to find any as the women had hidden it. It had been reported to Ehlert by Kopper that other prisoners were in possession of jewellery and when she did not find it she struck Kopper and told other prisoners to set about her. Kopper was hated by the other prisoners and they all began to beat her. Kopper had to be taken to hospital afterwards and I was told by other prisoners that she had a miscarriage when about four months pregnant.

I identify No 3 on photograph 37 as an SS woman who was an Aufseherin [Aufseherin] in Kitchen No. 1 at Belsen. I knew her by the name Ilse Forster. I often saw Forster beating other prisoners with a thick stick in the kitchen. She struck male prisoners across the head and women across the backside, but sometimes she hit women on the head too. I have seen Forster beat many prisoners until they were unconscious and they were then left lying bleeding on the floor. These beatings were inflicted in a room within the same building as the cookhouse and I saw the beatings through a window of the room. These beatings were given because prisoners asked for food or because they took food from the kitchen. I have seen unconscious,prisoners who had been beaten by Forster got free. I did not see all the shootings but I saw these dead bodies and their bullet wounds.

(Sworn by the said deponent Regina Bialek at Belsen this 15th day of June 1945.)

Regina Bialek, *deposition*[9]

(Deposition of Josef Rosensaft (male) late of Bendsburg, Modrow Str 62, Poland, sworn before Captain Alexander Mackinlay Forbes, Royal Artillery, Legal Staff, No. 1 War Crimes Investigation Team.)

I am a Polish Jew and 35 years of age. I was arrested on 27th August 1943 in Bendsburg and was brought to Auschwitz. I was eleven weeks in Auschwitz and then transferred to a camp nearby at Lagisa. I was there about 6.5 months when I escaped about the end of May 1944. I was recaptured in July 1944 and held in solitary confinement at Auschwitz until December 1944. I was then taken to a camp in the middle of Germany called Langen Salze where I was in a punishment company. I was there two months until the beginning of February 1945 when I was transferred to Dora and from there to Belsen on 10th April 1945. I came direct to Camp 2 and at that time the Hungarian soldiers were living in Camp 3.

Some days before the British came the Hungarians took over the guarding of the camp. They were working with the SS. I was living in Block 87 and between Block 87 and Block 86 there was a kitchen. Outside the kitchen there were bins in which the refuse of food was put. The Hungarians were all round the kitchen and there was also a Hungarian patrol walking round the camp.

The internees who were ravenously hungry were trying to get food out of the refuse bins and also potatoes through the kitchen cellar window. I saw the Hungarians shooting at the internees around the swill bins and the cellar with rifles and pistols. Many people fell and others ran away. I, with some of the internees, were detailed to remove the bodies of those who were dead and put them in a ditch near the kitchen. Those who were still alive were taken to the hospital. I know the names of two who were killed. These are, Slama Wolfowicz and Popowicz. The body of Wolfowicz I myself placed in the ditch. This shooting went on spasmodically throughout the 13th, 14th and 15th April 1945 whenever the internees tried to get food from the swill bins or the kitchen cellar. There were 77 killed in the three days and they all came from Blocks 86 to 91. I was careful to make a check of the figures of those killed because I thought the information might be useful as evidence if I ever got free. I did not see all the shootings but I saw these dead bodies and their bullet wounds.

(Sworn by the said deponent Josef Rosensaft at Belsen this 29th day of June 1945.)

Josef Rosensaft, deposition[10]

([Josef] Kramer – Camp Commandant at Belsen – statement 22nd May 1945 in 'Citadel' prison in Diest, Belgium)

I have heard of the allegations of former prisoners in Auschwitz referring to the gas chamber there, the mass executions and whippings, the cruelty of the guards employed, and that all this took place either in my presence or with my knowledge. All I can say to all this is that it is untrue from beginning to end.

[At Belsen] All prisoners received three meals a day [. . .] Apart from bread the rations were never cut down.

Josef Kramer, *former commandant at Belsen, statement*[11]

Accompanied by Lt. Col. Evelyn Smith of the Legal Division I drove to Lüneburg on September 17th to attend the opening session of the Belsen trial on the following day. Lüneburg is an attractive and undamaged Hanseatic town standing on the northern fringe of the famous heath, about 35 miles south east of Hamburg. [. . .]

The trial opened at 10 o'clock on the morning of September 18th [. . .] We took our seats in a fair-sized hall with a gallery round three sides. At one end was a cinematographic projector in a large black box, and at the other a screen. Desks for the press correspondents (said to number 200) were arranged under the projector; below them sat the four officers of the prosecution; to the right, along the side of the hall, sat the Military Court and behind them, the representatives of the United Nations; opposite the Court, on the other side of the hall, were the officers in charge of the defence, and behind them was the box reserved for the accused. At the other end, under the screen, were the interpreters (one for German and the other for Polish, as some of the accused are Poles), the shorthand-writers, the witness box and the official guests. When we arrived, the hall was already full of people – press correspondents of all ages and nationalities, including half a dozen Russians, and of both sexes; cameramen, military police, Court officials and spectators like myself. The galleries were occupied by a considerable number of civilians, who I was told were hand-picked Germans invited to witness the proceedings. Almost the only other civilian in the place was Dr Norman Bentwich, representing some Jewish organisation in the United Kingdom. The whole scene was brilliantly lit up, like a stage, by powerful electric lights.

Shortly before 10 o'clock, those present were informed by a loudspeaker that the Court was about to enter and that when it did so we should all stand up, wearing our hats. The Court entered – a Major-General, a Brigadier, four other officers and the Judge-Advocate, wearing the traditional wig. Then came the accused, some 25 men and 20 women, dressed in prison grey and wearing large numbers on their chests and backs, like runners in a cross-country race. Joseph Kramer was No. 1. The prisoners were escorted by a strong body of red-capped military police, male and female, who sat among them. With the exception of one of the women, who swayed as though she were about to faint, none of them betrayed any signs of emotion, and they remained calm and impassive throughout the proceedings. Some of them, but by no means all, were obviously of the criminal type, and on the whole the women struck me as being more sinister in appearance than the men. Kramer himself reminded me of a debased version of Rudolf Hess.

The President of the Court gave the photographers 20 minutes to flash their magnesium bulbs and whirr their cinematograph apparatus. They were then bidden to retire, and the Judge-Advocate read the Order convening the Court, and the names of the accused. He spoke in a curiously conversational voice, turning every now and then to the German or Polish interpreter for help when his powers of pronunciation failed him. The names of the prosecuting and defending officers were announced, and the Court, the shorthand-writers and the interpreters were sworn in. The first charge – that relating to Belsen – was then read out by the Judge Advocate and translated into both German and Polish.

It was then the turn of the defence, which consisted of about a dozen young officers not above the rank of major. Each of them was entrusted with the defence of about four of the accused. Their spokesman made two applications to the Court; the first was for the right to object at a later stage of the proceedings, that the charge had disclosed no offence, and the second was for the help of the Court in securing the attendance of Professor Lauterpacht of Cambridge University or Professor Brierly of Oxford University, or some other recognised authority on international law, on the grounds that points of international law arose on which the defence felt that they needed advice. The defence also produced a long list of witnesses whose presence they regarded as essential or desirable. They made it clear, however, that they did not propose to ask for an adjournment of the proceedings at this stage.

There followed an informal and friendly discussion between the defence and the Judge-Advocate, who assured them that they had the right to impugn the validity of the charges at any time if they wished to do so. The defence then went on to claim that the two charges and the various defendants named in them had been incorrectly joined and that it was unreasonable to describe the alleged misdeeds of the accused as having been 'concerted'. The uninitiated among the audience found this argument rather difficult to follow, as the second of the two charges – that relating to the notorious camp at Auschwitz (Oswiecim) in Poland – had not yet been read out. Moreover, the speakers were not always audible from where I sat owing to the noise of lorries and cars starting up their engines immediately outside the windows of the Court. There was a discussion in which the prosecution, hitherto silent, took a vigorous part; the Court adjourned for ten minutes, and returned to announce that the application of the defence for the severing of the charges could not be entertained. (Throughout the proceedings, the interpreters were used only when the accused were being directly addressed by the Court.)

The Court then adjourned for lunch. When it reassembled, the accused were asked singly whether they pleaded guilty or not guilty on both charges (the second of which was then read out). All pleaded not guilty. The case for the prosecution was then put by Lt. Col. Backhouse the senior prosecuting officer. In contrast with the defence, which gave the impression of being rather taken aback by the magnitude of the task thrust upon it only a few days before, and much in need of expert advice, Lt. Col. Backhouse spoke fluently and with assurance. He based his case on provisions of international law from which he quoted extracts. He then gave a lengthy description of the conditions found at Belsen by the first British officers to enter the camp on and after April 15th. He explained that, although he would produce one or two witnesses who had been inmates of the camp, most of the evidence would necessarily have to be submitted in the form of signed statements by the accused and affidavits taken from inmates before they were dispersed.

We learnt that Belsen was originally a small transit camp for political prisoners. In November 1944 Kramer, who was then in charge of a section of the much bigger camp at Auschwitz, was called to Berlin and informed that Belsen was to become a convalescent camp for sick people from other camps, displaced persons etc. He was appointed Commandant and took charge of Belsen on December 1st. He had volunteered for the SS in 1932, and had been concerned with the administration of concentration camps since that date. Most of his staff at Belsen had been his collaborators [in Auschwitz[12]]; one or two of them, and in particular the notorious Irma Grese, had originally been prisoners who had been promoted to positions of authority in accordance with the well-known Nazi policy, as Lt. Col. Backhouse described it, of appointing prefects to help the masters.

Thus ended the first day of the Belsen trial. I found my legal friends rather unhappy about the whole business; they remained unconvinced by the prosecution's contention that the alleged offences are indictable under international law, and were puzzled by the failure of the defence to demand an immediate decision on this fundamental issue. As a layman, I find it difficult to share their qualms. It seems to me all to the good that this remarkable state of affairs, in which it is possible for the defenders of Josef Kramer and his associates even to suggest that there is, in law, no case against them, should be brought home to the public in this way. I had never seen a British Military Court at work before; its proceedings are marked by a mixture of dignity and informality which, one feels, few other nations could achieve; and I left with the conviction that our prestige could only be enhanced by the spectacle of a body of very typical British officers, none of whom could by any means be described as a master of the forensic art, applying themselves with calm common-sense to the job of finding out the truth.

Cecil E. King[13]

We arrived in Lüneburg at 9 am, parked the wagon and walked across to the British Military Court House, which was barricaded off and guarded by armed British sentries in their red caps. Our official passes appeared to satisfy them and we were allowed to pass on to the main entrance, where they again produced the open sesame. We were shown into very good seats behind the witness box and had time to survey the court before the day's session opened.

[...]

German carpenters had converted a gymnasium into a courthouse to hold 250 of the public as well as the officials. The public gallery facing the accused was crowded with Germans who were listening to the revelations of the Concentration Camps with rapt attention. This gallery was closed in with wire netting. Some of these people, although Germans, had suffered under the Hitler regime. All Germans were searched before they entered the court and pocket knives, etc., removed in case they attempt to pass them for the prisoners to commit suicide. The German press was represented by nine men and I believe news of the trials is being given over the Hamburg Radio.

Seated in three-tiered rows, with the most notorious in the front, the prisoners were guarded by men and women of the British Military Police. There were forty-five prisoners in the dock, twenty-six men and nineteen women. I think three others on trial were ill and did not attend, because I saw one wearing No. 48. They were dressed either in old SS uniforms without badges or as civilians, and were the most menacing and degenerate-looking lot of human beings I've ever seen together. Obviously with a poor mental development. They filed in, some smirking, others stolid and sullen, and took their seats. Large black numbers on a white background were sewn on the backs of their garments and on cardboard hung round their necks in front. It is said that each of these accused is responsible for at least 1,000 murders.

[...]

That these men are given British justice is too fantastic and I'm sure they do not appreciate the privilege. I don't know how the twelve men for the defence can possibly do it, but, of course, they must, if selected, as they are all British army officials, except one Polish Lieutenant who is defending four of the Poles among the accused. Major T. C. M. Winwood defended Kramer, who with the other accused refused an opportunity to have German civilian counsel, whom they would have had to pay.

Muriel Knox Doherty, *Chief Nurse and Principal Matron,*
United Nations Relief and Rehabilitation Administration,
from letter dated 10 October 1945[14]

It was September, and the Lüneburg trial that I mentioned in my letter was the next big distraction from the endless waiting for the end to our domicile in Belsen. I was called as a witness. The trial struck me as a huge farce. I came face to face with British justice, under which you are innocent unless proven guilty, for the first time. This is no doubt a commendable principle, but it is difficult to apply or even adapt to the sort of crimes that were being dealt with in Lüneburg. I saw them there all lined up: Kramer (the Belsen Camp Commander), Klein (a doctor), Grese, the lot, and with them, admittedly at the end of the line, some of the Kapos [inmate functionaries] who had distinguished themselves by their bestial behaviour towards their fellow prisoners.

My command of the English language was reasonably good by then and I was able to dispense with an interpreter. First, I had to identify the prisoners. That was easy enough. (I wonder what went through Kramer's head when I identified him?) Then came the absurd aspect of the proceedings. For example, there were questions like: 'did you ever see any of these people kill anybody?' If you answered 'yes', the next question would be: 'which day of the week was this, and what time exactly?' Naturally you had to answer 'I don't know'. You were under oath, but in the camp you had neither a watch nor a calendar, nor would you have been the slightest bit interested whether it was Monday or Tuesday. That you simply could not answer such a question was enough to make you feel you were not telling the truth. It was hard for me to reconcile myself to the fact that these criminals actually had a counsel for their defence, just as in a normal British law court. That made me very angry indeed. So angry that I said there and then, in the witness box and under oath, that, while I was not defending the Kapos, I thought it entirely wrong that they should be tried alongside the people whose system had turned them into the animals they had become. The Kapos should have had their own separate trial. However, it had no noticeable effect. Most of the defendants were sentenced to death anyway. The whole trial was, as it happened, a wonderful opportunity for a lot of young barristers to display their ability to defend criminals. It was sick-making for the likes of us who had been at the receiving end of this murder machine. [. . .]

It was at that instant that I understood for the first time how incomprehensible to the rest of the world were the events which had led to the Lüneburg Trial. Is it possible to apply *law* in the conventional sense to crimes so far removed from the law as the massacre of millions of people, which were perpetrated in the cause of 'purifying the human race'?

Anita Lasker-Wallfisch, *survivor of Auschwitz and Belsen*[15]

It is all over now, and I shall have a bitter after-taste for a long time to come. It was not so much that one had to see these criminal types again and that one felt transported back into the past. I stood there, and I was asked questions, and as far as I am concerned I answered them more briefly and to the point than may have been strictly necessary. However much I racked my brain to describe things in greater detail and more effectively, I just could not do it in this overblown theatre. I spoke in English, which made a great impression, although what the witnesses looked like seemed to be of greater interest to these gentlemen than what they had to say. The *Daily Mirror* photographed me in a variety of poses [...]

> **Anita Lasker-Wallfisch**, *letter written by Anita to her cousin Heli,*
> *after her court appearance at the Belsen trial, from Lüneburg,*
> *dated 2nd October 1945*[16]

Deposition of Joszef Silberstein (male) late of 6 Str. Cloaks, Targu Murez, Romania, sworn before Major Thomas Humphrey Tilling, Royal Artillery, Legal Staff, No. 1 War Crimes Investigation Team.

I am 18 years of age and a Romanian. I was arrested in May 1944 and put in prison. After three weeks I was transferred to Auschwitz where I remained until the beginning of July 1944 and was then sent to Buchenwald. I only remained at this camp for a few days and I was then moved to two camps near Leipzig, first to Seitz and then to Bergoelster. I was then transferred back to Buchenwald in November 1944 and arrived at Belsen on 21st January 1945.

On 22nd August, 1945, in company with Lieutenant H. H. Alexander, Pioneer Corps, 21 Army Group Interpreters Pool, attached to No. 1 War Crimes Investigation Team, I visited Belsen Detention Cell and there recognised a man whom I knew as Isaak. I am now told that his full name is Isaak Judalewsky. He was a Capo in No. 1 Camp at Belsen.

I lived in the same Block as Judalewsky at Belsen, this was Block No. 2, and he was the Deputy Blockleader and Capo of the sleeping quarters. He pretended not to be a Jew and was extremely brutal in his treatment of the Jewish prisoners. I have seen him beating sick and half starved prisoners with the buckle part of his belt or a wooden board taken from the bed itself. These beatings were so serious that in my opinion they must have caused numerous deaths.

Before and after morning Appel he would go round the sleeping quarters and beat the sick people who were lying in their bunks unable to get up. He would beat them with the buckle part of his belt and whilst beating them he would drag them to the floor and continue to beat them. In many cases I have seen them left in an unconscious state on the floor. The hut orderlies would pick up the victims and put them back on the bed. Some days, when an internee doctor was present, he would examine the victims and, if still living, would put them back into their bunks or, if dead, have their bodies removed.

I remember an occasion when I was present at the beating of one of these prisoners which caused his death. About the middle of March I saw Judalewsky enter the sleeping quarters and he went to a sick prisoner on the top bunk. He struck him two violent blows with the buckle part of his belt on the mouth and face and the prisoner lept down from the bed and collapsed unconscious on the floor. Judalewsky continued to beat him with the belt for about 10 minutes and also kicked him with his boots. After he had left the room, I and several of my comrades went to fetch the internee doctor, Dr. Konig, who has since died of typhus, and after examining the man he told us the man was dead.

(Sworn by the said deponent Joszef Silberstein at Belsen this 29th Day of August 1945 before me)

Joszef Silberstein, *deposition*[17]

Taken at Belsen this 30th, day of August 1945 by the undersigned Major Thomas Humphrey Tilling, Royal Artillery, Legal Staff, No. 1 War Crimes Investigation Team.

Questioned: My name is Isak Judelewsky and I am 21 years of age. I am a Polish Jew. I was taken to the Ghetto at Bialistok in 1941 and remained there until 1942, when I was transferred to Lublin Concentration Camp. I have also been in Blizyn, Plasov, Gross Rosen and Buchenwald Concentration Camps. I arrived in Belsen in February 1945, and I became a Capo in Block No. 2

Charged: You are charged with the following offences:
  i) At Belsen, about the middle of March 1945, murder by beating a fellow internee until he died
  ii) Beating fellow internees at various dates at Belsen

[...]

Statement: About the man I have killed and the people I have beaten. I would like to know the name of the person whom I have killed as I do not know anything about having killed anyone.

I have beaten people, I agree, but only because it was necessary to keep the block clean when people refused to do it. For instance I saw a prisoner come in with dirty boots and he was going to bed in his boots. I asked him to take his boots off and I said 'The block must be kept clean and you must take off your boots'. He refused to do this so I had to beat him.

When the people made the block dirty by refusing to go to the lavatory I was woken up to restore order in the Block. The prisoners themselves asked me to restore order and I was afraid some SS Blockleaders would come and see it so I had to punish people like that. On another occasion one of the prisoners stole bread from another prisoner and I was asked to punish him because I was responsible for order in the block. I was always asked by the Blockleader to keep order and I was responsible for such order to the Blockleader and to the SS guards.

I have never beaten people because I am a sadist or because I liked it, but because I had to do it.

I would like you to help me and to let me free.

Isak Judelewsky, *a Belsen 'Capo', statement*[18]

NOTES

1. Donald Bloxham, *Genocide on Trial* (Oxford: Oxford University Press, 2001), pp. 18–19, 76–7.
2. Tony Kushner, *The Holocaust and the Liberal Imagination: A Social and Cultural History* (Oxford: Blackwell, 1994).
3. Bloxham, *Genocide on Trial*, pp. 66, 99.
4. United Nations War Crimes Commission, *Law Reports of Trials of War Criminals*, vol. 1 (London: HMSO, 1947), p. 93.
5. Bloxham, *Genocide on Trial*, pp. 97–101.
6. From 'Calling Australia', broadcast 30 October 1945, in Muriel Knox Doherty, *Letters from Belsen 1945* (Crows Nest, NSW: Allen & Unwin, 2000), p. 171. Republished with the permission of the Dimbleby estate.
7. Public Records Office Documents – WO309/1696.
8. Public Records Office (PRO), War Office (WO) 235/24.
9. PRO, WO 235/24.
10. PRO, WO 235/24
11. PRO, WO 235/24.
12. These two words appear in the draft version of this document but are obscured in the original.
13. PRO, Foreign Office 1049/237.
14. Muriel Knox Doherty, *Letters from Belsen 1945*, pp. 153–4, 162.
15. Anita Lasker-Wallfisch, *Inherit the Truth 1939–1945* (London: Giles de la Mare, 1996), pp. 124–7.
16. Ibid., p. 128,
17. PRO, WO 311/274.
18. PRO, WO 311/274.

Chapter 7
Facing Belsen: Remembrance and Memorialization

Shortly after the burning of the Belsen barracks, the lord mayor of nearby Hanover appealed to his fellow citizens:

> To make easier and more pleasant the life in the camp of these unfortunate victims of criminal actions, I call on the inhabitants of Hanover to donate books in every language, with the exception of the German language, also gramophones, records and other musical instruments...as well as recreational games...I am convinced that through their donations the population of Hanover – those whose property has been spared from the effects of war – will provide the proof that it has nothing in common with the now-defeated Nazi regime, and is prepared to help the pitiable victims of that regime as much as it has the power to do so.[1]

These aspirations were unrealistic. Solidarity with the victims had been in very short supply during the Nazi period. As for public awareness of the concentration camps, before 1939 they had been accepted and in some quarters even welcomed by a population willing to accept the Nazi line about sacrificing the civil liberties of a minority in the pursuit of an authoritarian but stable order. The false propaganda that depicted the camp inmates as criminals, antisocials, traitors, and threats to German peace and prosperity proved powerful and endured even as the camp network extended its functions and altered its targets during the war. The pleas of ignorance by populations in the vicinity of the camps – pleas detailed below in the accounts of Major Allan, Lord Molyneaux and Louis Kochane – were almost always convenient excuses developed on the German defeat.

Belsen holds a unique place in the British memory of the war. Conversely, in France, it is little known, with other institutions and places of suffering more prominent in the French consciousness. For the USA, the camps liberated by American troops at Dachau and Buchenwald held public attention. Equally, each of the Allied powers used the institutions it had liberated, which were generally within its zone of occupation, as an illustration to the German population of complicity and acquiescence in Nazi crimes. 'Das ist eure Schuld' – 'this is your responsibility' – was the explicit message imparted by the occupiers in the earlier stages of occupation when the emphasis was on the idea of collective German guilt for Nazism. (Interestingly, this was to be qualified as the Cold War began and the rhetoric of the Western Allies began to discriminate more between active Nazis and the rest of the German population, with the idea of the 'concentration camp' used to symbolize the victimhood of anti-Nazi Germans as well as 'racial' or 'social' 'enemies' of Nazism.) To that end, Germans were sometimes forcibly taken around the newly liberated camps, and even made to clean them. Although the typhus danger at Belsen prohibited extensive organized tours, as Allan, Lord Molyneaux and Kochane testify, Allied forces conducted some limited visits to impress the reality of the camp upon local Germans and dignitaries. Like other camps, Belsen became the subject of extensive newsreel footage and photograph exhibitions aimed at ordinary Germans.

With the final closure of the DP camp in autumn 1950, Belsen changed character again. It was now no longer a going concern, more an object of historical and political interest. Nevertheless, the developing memorial function of the camp and the concrete forms given to that memorialization give the observer an insight into the dynamic relationship between politics and history since the downfall of Nazism.

Christian survivors of Belsen swiftly erected a wooden cross at the edge of the mass graves. The provisional wooden monument created by the Jewish survivors was replaced in April 1946 by a permanent stone edifice. Later in 1946 the British military government decreed the creation of a place of commemoration on the site of the camp, including an obelisk and a memorial wall. Inaugurated in November 1952, this was transferred to the jurisdiction of the regional German civil authority (Niedersachsen/Lower Saxony). In 1966 a document centre and permanent exhibition on the fate of the Jews under Nazism were created; these facilities were further enhanced from 1985 to 1990 to create the institution as it is found today.

Another memorial was erected in June 1946 to the Soviet prisoners of war who had died of disease, exposure and famine in the first incarnation of the camp. Yet, and in all likelihood because of the onset of the Cold War, this memorial was situated at a distance from the main camp, and the murder of this group remains something of a blind spot in the memory of Belsen, as do the deaths of some 3.3 million Soviet POWs in German captivity in the Second World War. For equally regrettable political and cultural reasons the Sinti victims of the camp were not officially commemorated on the Belsen memorial wall until 1979.[2]

All of this goes to show the selectivity of 'memory', how it is impossible to fix objective meanings to memorials that will inevitably be 'read' in a subjective fashion. Much the same goes for the wider memory of Nazism and its crimes, as shown in the speech reproduced below given by Federal President Heuss at the 1952 memorial inauguration ceremony. This is an interesting example of German ambiguity at that time towards the Nazi past, and deserves a close reading in order to see the complex ways in which responsibility is simultaneously admitted and deflected. Particularly noteworthy are the absence of specifics of any sort, with the Holocaust touched upon but not detailed, the agency of the perpetrator left hanging and imprecise; the way in which crimes of other nations are touched upon, only, of course, to be swiftly discounted, except that they have already been brought to the listener's attention; and the veiled references to Nazism as an anti-Christian and anti-middle-class phenomenon as much as an antisemitic force.

*

I remember the CO [...] told everybody that we must be careful to contain our feelings and not to allow ourselves to become brutalised as the Germans had, and not to be unduly out of control, as it were. And I think everybody paid attention to that. It is true that we did make the Germans help to remove the bodies and so forth, but we had little option: they had to be removed and I think it was only fair that we did use them. [...] Very unwillingly the Wehrmacht, they were really affected themselves, I think. Whether some of the Germans actually knew what had been going on inside the camp or not, I don't know. [...] *We*, most certainly, could not believe it – and I really think in a way that *they* could not believe it. So how far that they had been inside the camp or not I don't know. I think we got some Wehrmacht prisoners in also who seemed really horrified at what they saw. [...] The Burgomasters of Celle and various towns roundabout were taken to the camp and shown one of the last pits to be filled in – and they of course were horrified. And we did get an awful lot of various help from them in the way of clothing and so on. But I think that they did not know either. The funny thing was – this place, on Lüneburg heath, beautiful surroundings, admittedly it was near a tank training school – but I think it was a place that was just not known of. The railway lines led straight to it, and I suppose the trains carrying the intended prisoners were driven there, and they were taken out of the trucks and they were just swallowed up, and nobody ever knew.
[...]

I'm not saying there was any kind of fraternal feelings towards the SS or the Wehrmacht even, but I think everything was extremely correct, extremely.

Major Alexander Smith Allan, *113 Light Anti-Aircraft Regiment*[3]

In spite of the fact that it is said the Panzer troops were forbidden to visit the SS guards at Camp No.1 and vice versa, one finds it difficult to believe that the horrors which existed in that camp were unknown to those living in the neighbourhood.

> **Muriel Knox Doherty**, *Chief Nurse and Principal Matron,*
> *United Nations Relief and Rehabilitation Administration,*
> *from letter dated July 1945*[4]

There must have been thousands of Germans who knew what was going on, but when we used to ask the German people if they knew about the concentration camps, they would say: 'Yes, we knew, and we were afraid that if we spoke out against the Government, we too would end up in them.' They knew what was going on, but they were only concerned about saving their own skins.

> **Gena Turgel**, *survivor of Auschwitz and Belsen*[5]

As the war was about to end our RAF Wing Headquarters 1309 reached the Luftwaffe Base near Lüneburg. Operational activities became fewer as targets reduced in number.

On a sunny afternoon our Commanding Officer Wing Commander R. E. H. Gould received instruction for us to escort a RAF Medical Unit to a liberated Concentration Camp which turned out to be Belsen. [...]

The entrance was manned by British Military Police who required us to disconnect all motor horns, explaining that any sudden sound would kill some of the many inmates wandering aimlessly in our path. [...]

On proceeding into the camp, we were warned to refrain from giving food to any inmates who would have died on the spot as their stomachs had shrunk with starvation. For us it was mental torture to resist the temptation to share with the inmates even our limited personal supply of biscuits and sweets. Our feeling on being faced with this terrible scene was best expressed in our Wing Commander's reflection: 'Did you ever imagine that one set of human beings could ever do this to another set of human beings?' [...]

Wing Commander Gould offered assistance in a back-up role and it was agreed that we explore the countryside with a view to obtaining blankets, bedding and clothing. In this we adopted a 'no red-tape' approach – going directly to call on the Lüneburg Burgomaster and his council, which was actually in session. A self-important official attempted to block our entry but when the Wing Commander drew his revolver the opposition collapsed and we strode into the Council Chamber.

At first the Burgomaster and his colleagues displayed arrogance and outrage, but on the sight of the drawn revolver and my loaded gun they decided to switch to ignorance of the Concentration Camp. Our response was to order them aboard our 3 ton lorry and force them to see for themselves. The shocking conditions of the inmates and the accommodation did not appear to surprise them but realising that the game was up they decided that cooperation was the safest option.

We dumped them back at their council offices and in their hearing we talked of the War Crimes Commission. This had the desired effect of the Burgomaster issuing orders to Council Staff and prominent citizens to make available everything on our want list. We very quickly organised a shuttle service which resulted in our Army Medical Colleagues being able to make life just a little better for the wretched inmates who had almost given up hope of survival.

Lord Molyneaux of Killead[6]

While we were stopped in Celle for a while, there was a rumour going around that there was a camp nearby where lots of people were incarcerated in deplorable conditions: a lot of Jews, mainly Jews as well. And I had been [. . .] reading the papers around there – because the war was supposed to be over – and there were stories of atrocities that the Germans had committed, and I remember nurses and various people I was talking to saying 'Oh, that's rubbish; it's just English propaganda, it's not true.' [. . .] So that stuck in my mind.

Then somebody said, 'Oh, there's a camp near here.' I said, 'well lets go and have a look at it.' So we got a truck, took the truck, and went there, and drove in. And then I saw bodies and people [. . .] and the mess and the stench, and all the things that were going on there. And this was the most horrifying spectacle.

So I remember going back to Celle. I think we went to the town hall or some sort of place, spoke to a lot of people, and said: 'You believe that the Germans did nothing during the war? You would like to see something? Come with us and we'll take you in the truck.' So we took them, put them in the truck, drove back there, drove in, and showed them. And they professed to be totally dumbstruck by the sight. [. . .] And their favourite saying was '[. . .] 'We knew nothing of it.' [. . .] 'We knew nothing at all about it' – 'Sometimes we heard trucks and things during the night, but we thought it was just ordinary army transport moving.' [. . .] They denied that they even knew of the existence of the place, and they must have seen smoke and lots of things, there; there must have been all sorts of things going around there. [. . .] I think they were civil servants or something or other, working in the town hall. Clerks – or whatever – whoever we could get to persuade, in one form or another, to come in the truck and go there. So just ordinary run of the mill people.

[. . .]

The authorities wouldn't have been too pleased that we were allowed to do this. We probably weren't allowed to do it of course. But I just said 'Come on, lets get the truck and have a look.' And by then the war was over and there wasn't a tremendous amount of authority anyway, so we could do all sorts of things.

[. . .]

We just took them in, showed them what we had seen – these wretched poor people in these terrible conditions – and said: 'This is your Germany, this is your proof. If you had denied that it could have happened, here it is, now you can see for yourself.'

Louis Kochane, *Jewish soldier in 8th Royal Tank Regiment,
7th Armoured Divivsion*[7]

When I was asked whether I would be prepared to say a word at this time and place I answered 'yes' without long reflection. For a 'no', indicating a refusal or an excuse, would have seemed to me cowardly and it is the will, the duty and the obligation of us Germans, as I see it, to learn to be brave in the face of the truth, especially on soil which has been both fertilized and laid waste by the excesses of human cowardice. For crude violence, endowed with rifles, pistols and batons, is when driven into a corner always cowardly, though when well-sated, threatening and pitiless, it may parade in the face of helpless poverty, sickness and hunger.

Anyone who speaks here as a German must possess the inner freedom to recognize the full cruelty of the crimes which were committed by Germans on this spot. It would be mere impudence to attempt to minimize them or to justify them by the misuse of the so-called 'raison d'état'.

Now I wish to say something which may astonish many of you but which I think many will believe though many who hear it over the radio [the speech was being broadcast on the radio] may not. I heard the word Belsen for the first time in the year 1945 in a BBC broadcast. I know that many in this country had a similar experience. We knew – or at least I knew – that Dachau, Buchenwald and Oranienburg were names that recalled no pleasant memories and over which a dirty brown stain had been smeared. Friends or relatives had told about it. Then the names of Theresienstadt, which at the beginning was so to speak prepared for visits by neutrals, and also that of Ravensbrück were heard. On one evil day I heard the name of Mauthausen where my old friend Otto Hirsch had been 'liquidated' – a noble and important representative of German Jewry in the Reich. It was his wife who told me of it and I tried to support and advise her. Belsen and Auschwitz were missing from this catalogue of terror and shame.

This remark is not intended to lend support to those who like to say that they knew nothing of what was going on. We *did* know about these things. We also knew from the writings of the Evangelical and Catholic Bishops, which found their way mysteriously to the people, of the systematic murder of inmates of German hospitals. This state, which regarded human feelings as a ridiculous and expensive form of sentimentality, wished to make a *tabula rasa* in this matter but their 'clean tables' bore traces of blood and ashes. Who cared? Our imaginations, which had drunk at the streams of middle-class and Christian tradition, could not grasp the volume of this cold and cruel destruction.

This Belsen and this monument stand for a historical destiny. This monument is erected to the sons and daughters of foreign nations, to German and foreign Jews but it is also a monument for the German people and not only for the Germans who are also buried in this soil.

I know that many ask themselves: was this monument necessary? Would it not have been better if the plough-shares had been driven across this field and the mercy of ever-renewed fertility had blotted out what had passed? In centuries' time a vague legend may grow up and relate of sinister happenings in this place. Good; let it be meditated upon. There is no lack of material such as fears that this obelisk may prove to be a thorn to prevent wounds healing through the passage of time.

Let us speak quite openly about it. Those who know that the bones of their own people lie here in common graves will be mindful of them, especially the Jews who were literally forced by Hitler into a sense of national consciousness. They never will and never can forget what was done to them and the Germans must not forget the deeds of men of their nation in those shameful years.

I hear the objection: what of the others? Have you never heard of the internment camps of 1945/46 and the brutality and injustice which was done there? Do you know nothing of the victims held in foreign custody; nothing of the suffering imposed by the formal yet cruel justice which even now holds German men in thrall? Are you unaware of the continued maltreatment and of the deaths which are taking place in the Soviet Zone in the camps of Waldheim, Torgau and Bautzen? Only the outward signs have changed.

I do know, and I have never hesitated to speak of these things. But to invoke the injustice and brutality of others in order to shield oneself is to adopt low moral standards. There are people who do this in other nations, among the Americans as well as the Germans, or the French or others. No nation is better than another; in every nation there are all kinds of men. America is not 'God's own country' and the harmless Emanuel Geibel did a certain amount of harm in a small way with his phrase: 'Am deutschen Wesen soll noch einmal die Welt genesen' ('The world shall again recover through the German way of life').

And would the Jews be the 'Chosen People' if they had not been especially set apart as victims of sorrow and suffering? It seems to me that the list of virtues with which the peoples provide themselves is a mean and corrupt affair. It endangers the clear and decent sense of patriotism which everyone who is sure of himself bears in him – that sense of patriotism which gives pride and security to those who see great things as they are and does not mislead them into the gloom of pharisaical self-confidence. Violence and injustice ought not to be used to reverse the balance on either side. Both bear within themselves the danger of cumulating in the consciousness of the soul; their weight becomes a sorry burden in the destiny of the individual and a still sorrier one in that of a people or peoples. All peoples have in reserve their prophets of revenge or, when these tire, their publicity men.

Here lie members of many nations. The inscriptions which we see are in various tongues. They are a document of the tragic distortion of European destiny. Here lie many German victims of terror and how many are there in other camps? There is deep significance in the fact that Nachum Goldman spoke here for all. For here in Belsen those Jews upon whom it was in any way possible to lay hands were intended to die of hunger or pestilence. Goldman spoke of the grievous path which the Jewish people had to tread and of its strength to meet the catastrophes of history. Certain it is that what happened between 1933 and 1945 was the most fearful experience which ever occurred to the Jews of the diaspora that later passed into history. In this something quite new happened and Goldman spoke of it. History has known many different kinds of persecution of the Jews. They were due in part to religious fanaticism and in part to a sense of social and economic competition. After 1933 there can be no question of religious fanaticism; to those who looked down with equal contempt upon the Holy Writings of the Old and the New Testament, the enemies of all religious feelings, this metaphysical problem was as foreign as it could be. The social-economic motive does not suffice unless it is merely interested in robbery after murder.

It was not only this, however. Basically there was something else. When the 'natural' behaviour of the semi-educated came to the fore, it led to murder as a purely automatic, pedantic, happening which did not even lay claim to a modest quasi-moral standard. This is the deepest corruption of the time. And it is *our* shame that such happenings should take place within the framework of that national history which brought Lessing and Kant, Goethe and Schiller into the world's conscience. Nobody can take this shame from us.

My friend Albert Schweitzer gave his teaching of natural ethics the title 'Respect for Life'. This formula is certainly the right one, however cruelly paradoxical it may seem to quote it in a place where it was ten thousand times held up to scorn. But does it not require supplementing by the words 'Respect for Death'?

I should like to relate a little story that may well displease many Jews and many non-Jews. On both sides they will say that it is irrelevant that in the first World War 12,000 German men of Jewish faith met their death for the German fatherland. In the memorial tablet in the town from which I come, these names figured in bronze letters among the names of all the other fallen comrades, comrade lying by comrade, inseparable. The local National Socialist party leader had the names of the Jewish dead scratched out and the spaces filled with the names of battles. I am not mentioning this because the names of boyhood friends of mine were removed. What was worst of all was my realization with horror that respect for death, the simple death of a soldier, had disappeared whilst new wars were being thought out.

Death in war and by war took the most fearful forms. Here in Belsen, war reigned with hunger and pestilence as its unpaid helpers. A cynic or a profligate might say that, after all, they were only Jews, Poles, Russians, French, Belgians, Norwegians, Greeks and so on. Only? They were men like ourselves; they had parents, children, husbands and wives. The pictures of those who survived are the most terrible documents.

Where this piece of land was concerned the war was over in April 1945 but deaths continued to come about from hunger and pestilence. British doctors lost their lives. But I have been asked by prominent Jews during the last few days to say a word about this epilogue and about the rescue by German doctors in the spring and early summer of 1945 of human beings marked out for death. I knew nothing about these things. I have however been told how at that time and in the face of such misery the will to help grew into self-sacrifice and how the physician's sense of duty and shame and fear of failing when faced with such [a] task led to Christian and sisterly devotion to those in danger who are indeed our 'neighbours'. I am thankful that I was told this and that this request was made to me. For in such vindication of what is directly right and good there lies a consolation.

The British Land Commissioner spoke of Rousseau. He began one of his books with the apodictic statement: 'Man is good'. We have learned that the world is more complicated that the theses of moralising writers. But we know this too: Man and Mankind are abstract assumptions, statistical assertions, often only vague phrases; but humanity itself is an individual line of conduct, a vindication of the self towards others, of whatever religion, race, standing and profession they may be. Let this be a consolation.

There stands the obelisk, there stands the wall with its multilingual inscriptions. They are of stone, cold stone. *Saxa loquuntur*: stones can speak. It depends on the individual, it lies with you to understand their language – for your own sake and for the sake of all.

First President of the Federal Republic of Germany Theodor Heuss,
translated version of speech at the ceremony at Belsen in 1952[8]

I have the honour to report that the memorial to the victims of the concentration camp at Belsen was dedicated there on Sunday, November 30th. The ceremony was originally supposed to take the form of a handing over of the memorial and the site of the camp to the Government of the Land of Lower Saxony, but in consideration of the feelings of those survivors of the camp, or relatives of victims, who were to be present, it was decided to confine the proceedings to the informal laying of wreaths, the repetition of prayers by Jewish, Catholic and Protestant ministers of religion, and speeches by Dr Nahum Goldmann, the Federal President and myself. It was also agreed that the British military band which was to be present should play no national anthems whatever, to avoid the playing of 'Deutschland über Alles' on such an occasion, and that the national flags of all countries the nationals of which died at Belsen should be flown on a row of poles standing in a circle surrounding the obelisk which is one of the main features of the memorial. This last arrangement made it possible to include the German national flag [. . .] without giving offence.

Representatives of Jewish organisations interested in Belsen were at first distressed at the suggestion that the memorial and the graves of the dead should be taken over by the Government of Lower Saxony and that the latter should assume responsibility for the ceremony on November 30th. They eventually however accepted the British argument that it was most important to bring home to the German people their share in the guilt of the Nazi regime; and that in consequence where a German Land Government was willing to make the gesture of organising the ceremony and taking over the memorial, it should on no account be snubbed. I was however most earnestly begged to see to it that the British authorities continued to interest themselves in the Belsen site and its proper protection in the future.

The dedication ceremony was originally supposed to take place in August. It had however to be postponed because the memorial was damaged by lightning. One might have assumed that the German authorities would have waited until next spring before holding an outdoor meeting in so bleak a spot, but I am told in confidence that the Foreign Ministry insisted that the ceremony should take place now, apparently for the sake of German–Israeli relations. They were also, I believe responsible for the great attention shown to Israeli feelings in such matters as the order of laying of the wreaths.

Most of the site of the concentration camp at Belsen is now covered with plantations of young conifers and birches, as yet only three or four feet high, except where the great neatly turfed mounds lie, each with a notice board in front of it saying 'Here lie 1,500 dead,' or 'Here lie 5,000 dead'. In the distance is a peaceful landscape of heaths and woods. It is quite impossible for a newcomer to recreate in his imagination the Belsen of 1945. Yet on Sunday the small gathering of deeply moved men and women standing in the snow under a grey sky and in piercing cold was not unimpressive. I heard German officials muttering to each other in distaste at the manners of the Belsen survivors, who crowded round the obelisk, jostling the President of the Republic and other dignitaries in their desire to take a full part in the proceedings; but to my mind their evident emotion gave meaning and life to what would otherwise have been only a formal official observance.

Because of the intense cold, only the laying of wreaths and the religious ceremonies took place at the memorial. Suitable music (not including 'Deutschland über Alles' despite the report in the Times of December 1st) was played by the Band of the Rifle Brigade. The entire gathering then adjourned to a large hall in the neighbouring British barracks at Hohne for the speeches. [...]

Dr Nahum Goldmann [...] had what was probably the first opportunity since the late war for a leading representative of world Jewry to address the German people. It is not surprising, therefore, that he made a vigorous statement and dwelt at length on the fate of the millions of Jews who had been 'coldly and systematically exterminated in gas chambers and other institutions of destruction'. At the same time he could easily have used more violent language and his speech seemed to show a desire not to stir up unnecessary hatred and ill-feeling despite its outspokenness. [...]

President Heuss spoke with admirable courage and frankness, and indeed said everything which one could possibly expect of a German representative on such an occasion. [...]

There is unfortunately no doubt that many of the German officials present found the proceedings distasteful. Members of my staff who have discussed President Heuss's speech with numbers of ordinary citizens have found that the latter had difficulty in reconciling their half-dormant anti-Semitism with what the President said about German guilt.

Hanover Land Commissioner, letter dated 5 December 1952,
addressed to Sir Ivone Kirkpatrick, UK High Commissioner,
(22c) Wahnerheide, Rheinland[9]

NOTES

1.   Reported in the *Neue Hannoverscher Kurier*, 5 June 1945, reproduced in Niedersächsische Landeszentrale für politische Bildung (ed.), *Konzentrationslager Bergen-Belsen: Berichte und Dokumente* (Hanover: Niedersächsische Landeszentrale für politische Bildung, 1995), p. 204.
2.   Ibid., pp. 235–6, 275.
3.   IWM Sound Archive 11903/2.
4.   Muriel Knox Doherty, *Letters from Belsen 1945* (Crows Nest, NSW: Allen & Unwin, 2000), p. 44.

5. From Gena and Norman Turgel, *I Light a Candle* (London, Grafton 1987), p. 110.
6. Account based on interview with Ben Flanagan.
7. Account based on interview with Ben Flanagan.
8. Public Records Office Documents – FO 371/98020.
9. Public Records Office Documents – FO 371/98020 (C1851/16).

Chapter 8
The Belsen Camp in Historical Context

Jo Reilly and Donald Bloxham

Belsen was but one site in a huge National Socialist concentration camp system that spread across Europe. It became infamous after its liberation in April 1945, when the sight of thousands upon thousands of emaciated and exhausted prisoners dumped there and left to die by the Nazis in the last six months of the war brought international condemnation. But who were these prisoners? How had they arrived at the camp? What was the role of Belsen in the wider Nazi system? Indeed, how and why did the Nazis introduce such a camp system? This chapter sets out to answer these questions. By no means an exhaustive narrative, the following pages present a general outline of the development of the camp system in the 'Third Reich' and Belsen's place within that system. The unique development of the Belsen site is examined from its conception in 1942 through to its evolution into the 'horror' camp that so shocked the British troops who entered it on 15 April 1945.

DEFINING THE ENEMY

The major domestic aim of Nazism was the creation of a new and unified national ethnic community – *Volksgemeinschaft* – based on both Teutonic myth and nineteenth-century race theory. Nazi ideology sought to rid German society of its perceived impurities and thus persecuted those who did not conform to the new ideal of the 'healthy', 'productive' 'Aryan' race, as well as ideologically problematic elements. People of the same 'Blood, Race and Soil' would together restore Germany to greatness. Ideological enemies – for example, communists and Jehovah's Witnesses – and 'asocials' – for example, 'habitual criminals' and, according to some definitions, Romanies – were regarded as a threat to the purity of the Volk and in need of political re-education by means of a period in a detention centre. Some groups, in particular Jews, Slavs, Blacks, and, again Romanies, were, it was claimed, fundamentally inferior, and therefore beyond re-education. Jews (and

'Judaeo-Bolshevism', for Jews and communism were often linked in Nazi propaganda) were portrayed as the most pernicious form of evil: a racially debilitating, corrupting element that conspired internationally in the pursuit of world domination.

In order to facilitate their political programme of isolation of their 'enemies', the Nazis required machinery far removed from the bureaucracy and judiciary inherited from the Weimar Republic. Thus, immediately upon the proclamation of Hitler as Chancellor in 1933, a series of decrees effectively gave legal authorization to arbitrary and unlimited detention. In particular, the 28 February Law for the Protection of the People and the State served as a basis for 'protective custody' (*Schutzhaft*), a term adapted to meet the requirements of the Nazi regime. Initially, members of the German Communist Party, Social Democrats and trade unionists suffered most as a result of the decrees. By the end of 1933 there were almost 30,000 people in 'protective custody' in a decentralised prison camp system, many the victims of unofficial or so-called 'wild' arrests by the SS (*Schutzstaffeln*), the elite Nazi defence corps, or the SA (*Sturmabteilung*), the brown-shirted paramilitary wing of the Nazi Party. The 'Enabling Act' of March 1933 allowed Hitler to pass laws without the consent of Parliament and from then on the formation of new political parties and the existence of trade unions became illegal.

THE CONCENTRATION CAMP SYSTEM IN THE 1930s

In effect the 1933 promulgations laid the ground for the establishment of the first concentration camps. The camp system expanded and the head of the SS, Heinrich Himmler, centralized the administration of the camps under its auspices. Eventually, prisoners in protective custody were concentrated in a small number of SS-run camps, the largest of which was Dachau, established in March 1933 near Munich in Bavaria. Furthermore, the original rationale of the camps – to provide 'political education' – was effectively superseded and the prisoners were subjected to torture and hard labour in a system of orchestrated, calculated brutality.

The year 1936 was key in the development of the SS and the camps, featuring the extension of the power of Nazi radicals in Germany as against that of the traditional elites. Himmler was established as chief of the German police, and the addition of this office to his leadership of the SS was an important fusion of the authority of party and state. He now had an official function in the Ministry of the Interior, which was critical for the success of his programmes of mass incarceration in the concentration camps. He could thus spread his net wider than ever in the pursuit of 'enemies' of the regime, and was aided in the task by further restrictive legislation.

Numbers in the camps swelled by several hundred per cent as new inmates were imprisoned during 1937–38. So-called habitual and professional criminals were incarcerated by the thousand, as were 'asocials' and the 'work-shy'. In 1939 the six major camps existing by that time in the Reich – Dachau, Sachsenhausen, Mauthausen, Flossenbürg, Buchenwald and Ravensbrück (the camp for women) – held over 21,000 internees. Prior to the end of 1938, however, comparatively few of these prisoners were Jews – perhaps a few thousand imprisoned as part of the campaign against the 'work-shy'.

POLICY AGAINST THE JEWS

In the pre-war period, as later, Nazi policy towards the Jews was a central facet of the regime. Yet that policy was in the first instance directed less at imprisoning Jews and more at stigmatizing, socially ostracizing and impoverishing them, and ultimately encouraging their emigration. Four hundred anti-Jewish laws were passed in the 'Third Reich'. Throughout the 1930s the civil and human rights of the German Jewish population (or at least those arbitrarily defined as such in the racial laws) were eroded. In 1935 the Nuremberg Laws deprived German Jews of their citizenship and proclaimed marriage and sexual relations between Jews and 'Aryans' illegal. Jews lost their right to vote and were removed from schools, universities and certain professions, and were progressively dispossessed of any business interests.

The year 1938 proved to be a watershed in the treatment of the Jewish population. In March the *Anschluss*, the occupation of Austria, brought a further 185,000 Jews into the Reich; they were immediately subject to the German anti-Jewish laws. On the night of 9–10 November, using as a pretext the murder of a German Embassy official in Paris by a Jewish student, Josef Goebbels, with Hitler's tacit consent, ordered that reprisals be taken against the German Jewish community. In a night of extreme violence across Germany known as *Kristallnacht* ('the night of broken glass'), synagogues were burned, Jewish shops and houses destroyed and many individuals killed. An estimated 30,000–35,000 Jews were placed in concentration camps following the pogrom. Many were subsequently released, but only on agreeing to emigrate, leaving any assets behind; 1,000 lost their lives.

For the first time, Jewish prisoners became a significant percentage of those incarcerated in the camps. What is more, they were imprisoned for no other reason than being Jewish. The violence and ferocity of *Kristallnacht* shocked the German population in a way previous anti-Jewish action had not. Yet following the outrage, the position of the Jews in German society became only further eroded as thousands were forced to leave the country. Those Jews who remained in Germany at the outbreak of war undoubtedly faced an uncertain future. None, however, could have been prepared for what was to come.

Within two years of war, the Nazi regime was in a position to begin the systematic murder of parts of eastern European Jewry and then the whole of the Jewish population in Europe. In Poland the Jewish population had already been subjected to tremendous deprivation. They had been forced to move into overcrowded ghettos where rations were at starvation levels. They were joined by Jews deported from Germany, Austria and Czechoslovakia. Thousands died from disease and malnutrition. In June 1941 the Soviet Union was invaded, and a new phase of escalation in Nazi Jewish policy began.

GENOCIDE

Alongside the military invasion, mobile squads of the SS and police were dispatched with a broad, racist 'security' remit that encompassed the killing of Jewish men of military age among other supposed threats to the consolidation of German rule. In hindsight, these first killings can be seen as the beginning of the 'final solution' in its 'final' form.

As Peter Longerich points out, Nazi Jewish policy as it had progressed up to 1941 clearly entailed the demise over the medium term of all Jews in the German sphere of power. Previous plans for massive Jewish 'reservations', either in the Lublin district of Poland (occupied in 1939) or (following the defeat of France in 1940) in the former French colony of Madagascar, would have led to a high death rate among the Jews dispatched to live in the harsh, overcrowded conditions of these inadequately resourced regions.[1] However, the precise course of developments underlying the escalation of Nazi policy over the months from June 1941 is still a matter of dispute. The probability is that at the outset of the invasion of the USSR deportation to the east (to beyond the Ural mountains) was the planned fate of the European Jews, with orchestrated murder at the reception points not yet envisaged. Soviet Jews were being killed in increasingly large numbers, though, so it is probably accurate to view the murder of the Soviet Jews, Jews from different areas of Poland, and Jews from Germany and the rest of Europe as, respectively and in that order, the result of different decisions or impulses at different times. Each phase represented a further expansion of the killing programme in accordance both with a self-radicalizing 'consensus' between the Nazi leadership in Berlin and its SS, police and even military operatives in the field, and with wartime circumstances.

What may be said with certainty is that beginning in August and September 1941, women and children were also murdered in increasing numbers in Soviet territory, and from September to October (and in Lithuania even from August), whole communities were targeted: clearly by this time the Soviet Jews were all slated to die in the immediate term. Mid-September also saw Hitler's decision to deport German Jews eastward, a policy that was implemented from October 1941. Once again, there is no scholarly unanimity as to whether there was a discernible intent in the first instance to kill all of these Jews outright and swiftly, although many of course perished as a result of the local conditions. Rather, the prime victims of orchestrated killing policies were those native to the areas to which German and other central and western European Jews were deported.

The first centres for mass killing by gas – a method drawing on previous German expertise in murdering the 'disabled', and introduced on practical and psychological grounds as less taxing for the killers – were possibly established for such regional purposes. In late September or early October 1941 construction began on a killing centre at Chelmno near Lodz in the western area of Poland annexed to the Reich (the Reichsgau Wartheland). In November construction began on the killing centre Belzec in the aforementioned Lublin district of central Poland (the administrative unit entitled the *Generalgouvernement*). The policy of killing in both regions was continually expanded over the following months.

A policy of instant murder of whole transportations of the vast majority of Jews deported into Poland fully crystallized between March and May 1942. In accordance, for instance, with discussions at the Wannsee conference of 20 January 1942, aspects of a slower 'death-by-attrition' policy remained, but the emphasis was very heavily now on the outright murder of all categories of Jews everywhere, under the radical leadership of Reinhard Heydrich of the SS Reich Security Head Office. The murder system reached its apex in the industrialized killing at Auschwitz-Birkenau.

In general terms, shooting by the SS and police squads accounted for up to two million Jews killed in the Soviet territories and parts of eastern Poland, while Belzec and two other extermination centres at Sobibor and Treblinka were used to murder the Jews of central Poland and other areas in the east. Auschwitz consumed the majority of the Jewish communities of western, central and southern Europe.

A COMPLEX CAMP SYSTEM

The existence of a concentration camp system does not mean that we can generalize carelessly about the administration and functioning of all the camps. The war effort demanded a massive increase in the number of people who were herded into the camps as forced workers. Additional labour camps and transit camps were established in the occupied territories by the local SS and police leaders, or even the civilian authorities or the German army, often independently of the existing camp network. There were hundreds of Nazi camps, sub-camps and factories employing slave labour. This remained the case even after February 1942, when the organization of all the various camps was finally consolidated and centralized under the SS Business Administration Main Office (WVHA), headed by SS General Oswald Pohl.

The regime and the conditions faced by the prisoners could vary enormously. Thus the 'pure' killing centres of Belzec, Sobibor and Treblinka remained under the authority of the SS and Police leader in central Poland, Odilo Globocnik. They were not really camps at all – more simple slaughterhouses – so, unlike Auschwitz and the other twin extermination-concentration camp facility at Majdanek (both of which camps were under Pohl's jurisdiction), they never accommodated masses of slave labour. Moreover, camps did not remain static but developed and changed as the National Socialist regime required. Initially, for instance, the original facilities of the Auschwitz camp served as a prison for Polish political prisoners.

Of all the camps, labour and prison camps were the most prevalent. In these places the type of work and the conditions could vary from one to the next, but they served the same end: to exploit human labour to the utmost for the minimum economic output. The real costs were paid in ineffable human suffering. As the German war machine came under increasing pressure, the need for forced labour in order to increase productivity became greater. At the same time, however, the machinery of the 'final solution' demanded more victims. In Auschwitz, then, when the trainloads of Jews arrived, selections were made on the platform: the children, the aged and those unfit for work were sent immediately to the gas chambers; those who were relatively fit and healthy were allowed a temporary reprieve, instead to be worked, in all likelihood, to death for the benefit of the German war machine.

THE LAST MONTHS OF THE WAR

In a report dated 15 August 1944, the WVHA stated that the number of concentration camp inmates was 524,286 (compared with 224,000 a year earlier and despite terrific mortality rates). This figure continued to increase. German troops were retreating on all fronts and fervent attempts were made to accelerate arms production. More workers were forcibly recruited and employed in underground factories. Furthermore, in the last months of the war thousands of prisoners, in order that they did not fall into Soviet hands, were marched from the camps in the east towards concentration camps in Germany.

Before the enemy approached, Himmler had ordered that the remaining killing centres be dismantled. Treblinka, Sobibor and Belzec had already been destroyed. Chelmno was liquidated in January 1945. During the latter part of 1944, only one extermination camp was still operating at full capacity:

Auschwitz. On 25 November, Himmler ordered the dismantling of the killing stations there too, and on 17 January 1945 he ordered a full-scale evacuation of those prisoners still remaining. When the Soviets reached the camp on 27 January 1945, they found only 2,000 inmates, the majority Jews and most too ill to move; the SS guard had fled, having failed to destroy all traces of the camp. Camps within German territory were evacuated in the face of advancing Soviet troops. In February, Gross Rosen in Silesia was evacuated and the prisoners moved further west to Buchenwald. Forced marches of prisoners also left Sachsenhausen and Ravensbrück.

The threat of Soviet arrival, then, did not result in the emancipation of thousands of prisoners, but rather precipitated the death marches of the winter of 1944–45. Prisoners were moved in their thousands on long marches lasting several days or weeks in freezing conditions and without adequate clothing or food. Those who collapsed were shot or left to die where they lay. Many were loaded on to trains but their lot was hardly easier. People were packed tightly, often into open cattle cars with no sanitary provision, and taken on long journeys constantly threatened by Allied bombing raids. At least a third of the more than 700,000 concentration camp inmates recorded in January 1945 lost their lives on the death marches and in the catastrophically overcrowded reception camps in the months before the end of the war.

BERGEN-BELSEN

Bergen-Belsen was one such reception camp, situated near Hanover in north-west Germany. In contrast to the extermination centres in the east, which when liberated by the Soviets were deserted except for those Jews who had been deemed incapable of leaving, Belsen, on 15 April 1945, held an estimated 61,000 emaciated and dangerously ill people crowded together in frightful conditions.

Few historians writing on Belsen have failed to point out the irony of the fact that following two years' existence as a relatively lenient camp for privileged prisoners it should have become in April 1945 one of the representative examples of the evils of the National Socialist regime. Eberhard Kolb, a historian of Belsen, believes it is only an apparent paradox, however, and argues that the development of Belsen from a detention camp into the 'inferno' where thousands lost their lives in 1945 was not inadvertent but instead reveals something of the mentality behind the concentration camp system. In his work, Kolb seeks to show that the Bergen-Belsen camp was firmly integrated into the Nazi system of oppression. In fact, at no point in the camp's history could conditions have been described as satisfactory; at best, life in Belsen was relatively endurable, at worst it was totally unbearable.[2]

AN 'EXCHANGE' CAMP IS DEVISED

Nevertheless, Belsen from its inception did hold a position in the camp system that was peculiar. It was established, unlike any other camp, in order to house a special group of Jewish prisoners who, it was envisaged, might be utilized in a diplomatic exchange plan. Aspects of the history of Belsen towards the end of the war reveal that, rather like the expanded initiative for a greater exploitation of Jewish slave labour,[3] the Nazi leadership was prepared to make small but real concessions to pragmatism in an otherwise ideologically driven system. Put simply, the leading Nazis 'certainly wished to eliminate the Jewish "race", but that objective did not rule out making limited exceptions to the general policy if there were sufficiently strong reasons to do so'.[4]

During 1941 and 1942 negotiations took place between the British and German governments which resulted in the exchange of Palestinian nationals, trapped in Europe by the onset of hostilities, for a number of German citizens. Primary among these was a group of Templars, an orthodox Lutheran sect, who years before the war had made their home in Palestine but now wanted to return to Germany. Two successful exchanges were executed in Istanbul with the help of the British Legation in Switzerland and the Jewish Agency in Palestine, the first in December 1941 and the second eleven months later. The precedent was set.

In mid-1942 officials in the German Foreign Office arrived at the idea that further exchanges might be possible, particularly of notable Jews. With Himmler's consent, an agreement was reached between the Foreign Office and the SS that 30,000 Jews would be held back from the transports to the death camps and detained in order that they might be exchanged for ethnically or politically 'valuable' Germans living in Allied countries, particularly those who had been interned by Britain or the United States. The selection of the Jews was based on one of three main criteria: those with important connections abroad; those whose fate was of enough concern to outsiders that they could be used to put political or economic pressure on the Allies; and prominent figures in public service. Indeed, aspects of the plan for holding Jews for potential exchange were developed from earlier German notions of holding Jews as hostages against the USA prior to the latter's entry into the war.[5]

After obtaining a concession from Hitler in December 1942, Himmler ordered the construction of a special camp in order to house these 'exchange Jews' (*Austauschjuden*). The WVHA located a suitable site near Hanover. In 1941 the area had been established as a camp for Soviet prisoners of war. Like the other Soviet POWs, these were simply left to starve to death in open-air enclosures. Possibly 18,000 died on the Belsen site alone, with more than 30,000 others perishing in three nearby camps.

THE BELSEN 'EXCHANGE' CAMP IS CREATED

The area now given over to the WVHA had been neglected so, during the summer of 1943, 500 slave labourers were brought in to rebuild the camp. They continued to be accommodated in what was named the Prison Camp (*Häftlingslager*), the first of several sub-camps eventually established. Here the prisoners lived in probably the worst conditions of the whole complex, enduring great deprivation and hard labour.

The name Bergen-Belsen appeared officially for the first time in a circular in April 1943. In March, Ernst Kaltenbrunner, successor to Reinhard Heydrich as chief of the Reich Security Head Office, had officially decreed the exemption of certain Jews from murder.

The first 'exchange Jews' – 2,500 Poles – arrived in Bergen-Belsen in two transports in July 1943 and were housed in isolation in the so-called Special Camp (*Sonderlager*). A year later all except 350 had been deported to Auschwitz. As future arrivals at the camp were to discover, the future in Belsen was no more certain than in any other camp. Many of those sent to their deaths had held Latin American papers – often simply a letter from a foreign consul guaranteeing citizenship rather than an actual passport. A large number of these papers were probably of dubious provenance. The sale of forged documents became a lucrative business in Europe and Gestapo agents were known to be involved; certainly, a significant traffic in Honduran and Paraguayan papers was uncovered in Switzerland. Often even those people who were legally entitled to these papers were forced to pay huge amounts of money to unscrupulous consular representatives who saw an opportunity to make money for themselves.

Those Poles who remained in the Belsen camp held *bona fide* documents. In the summer of 1943 they were joined by 367 Spanish Jews and 74 Greek Jews, all brought from Salonika. Though living in Greece, the 367 were Spanish nationals and as such were placed in a new sub-camp, the Neutral Camp (*Neutralenlager*). They were later joined by other small transports of Spanish, Portuguese, Argentinian and Turkish Jews. Conditions here were reasonably good and the prisoners were not subjected to hard labour. In February 1944 the Spanish Jews from Salonika left Belsen for Spain, eventually reaching Palestine.

The Greek Jews, meanwhile, were placed in a large section of the camp, which became known as the Star Camp (*Sternlager*). From the early months of 1944, they were joined by a large number of Dutch 'exchange Jews' deported from the transit camp at Westerbork. The first of eight transports left Westerbork on 11 January and by September a total of 3,670 people had been transferred to the Star Camp in Belsen. Thus the number of exchange prisoners in the Star Camp rose in seven months from under 400 on 1 January 1944 to over 4,000 on 31 July.

A great many of the 'exchange Jews' arrived in family groups and although men and women in the Star Camp were segregated at night, they were allowed to mix during the day. Work was mandatory in this camp. The prisoners were divided into work parties, the largest of which was the shoe 'commando'. Here the labourers were required to take apart thousands of old pairs of shoes and boots that had been delivered to Belsen from all over Germany as part of a winter relief collection. The re-usable leather was to be salvaged and sorted. Men, women and children worked for long hours in filthy conditions, constantly supervised by abusive SS guards. Imprisonment and the withholding of food rations were the punishments for not meeting work quotas.

The Star Camp was also known as the 'Albala Camp', after the Greek Jewish elder, Jacques Albala. He headed the Jewish Council, which was formed in April 1944, and was invested by the camp authorities with the right to impose punishments on his fellow prisoners. The other council members were drawn from the Greek and Dutch communities. There was even a Jewish court with an appointed judge and lawyer who sentenced prisoners to periods of detention in a cellar for misdemeanours such as stealing.

During the first half of 1944 life was bearable but very basic. Food consisted mainly of coffee, soup, bread and margarine and the staple food, turnip. Hunger was always a problem. Sanitary conditions were primitive, and there was no privacy. One section of the camp was converted into a hospital area by the prisoners, but there were very few medicaments available and the level of care that could be effectively administered was restricted. Cultural activities were pursued as much as was practicable. Prisoners tried to teach the children formal lessons and more general lectures and discussions were organized. On Fridays they sang Hebrew songs and an effort was made to celebrate the festivals. Life was hard, but for the majority faith in the exchange plan provided the strength to go on.

After the Star Camp, another sub-camp was formed in Belsen. Following the German military takeover in Hungary on 19 March 1944, during the ensuing massive assault on the Hungarian Jewish population, the Hungarian Camp (*Ungarnlager*) was established and in July 1,683 Jews were brought in. They were treated reasonably well and were not required to work. These people were in fact pawns in the complicated negotiations that were taking place between Himmler and Jewish organisations in the later stages of the war; the plan was to attempt to trade these few Jewish lives for money and war *matériel*.

Despite the original intentions of the German Foreign Office and the immense bureaucracy involved in implementing the scheme, the actual number of 'exchange Jews' held in Belsen who gained their freedom through genuine exchange was only 358. On 12 July 1944, 222 people from Belsen, together with a smaller number from the Vittel camp in France, reached Palestine in an exchange negotiated between the British and German governments. This was only a small number of the 'exchange Jews' in Belsen; it might have been more had the British been able to locate more German citizens who were suitable for exchange than was ultimately the case. In another exchange, 136 people holding South and Central American papers were taken from Belsen to safety in Switzerland in January 1945. Meanwhile, the majority who were not chosen for exchange began to lose hope. The Belsen exchange camp continued to function yet, during 1944, the site as a whole changed quite dramatically, in terms of both its role and its appearance.

A CHANGE OF ROLE

The WVHA decided that Belsen was being under-utilized. In March 1944 the Prison Section of Belsen was designated as a reception camp for the sick prisoners from other labour camps and factories under Pohl's control. The name given to this sub-camp – the Recuperation Camp (*Erholungslager*) – proved to be a euphemism. When the first transport of 1,000 men with tuberculosis arrived from Dora in March 1944, no attempt was made to restore them to health. They were placed in empty barracks without blankets, mattresses or hot food, and received no medical attention. The high mortality rate in this camp reflected the conditions.

The evacuation of the eastern camps and the movement of thousands of prisoners inside German territory placed an enormous pressure on the existing concentration camps. Owing to its location, Belsen was chosen as a destination for the death marches. Besides, the German war machine could no longer afford the existence of a detention centre: Belsen was gradually transformed into a concentration camp proper. As we have seen, the conditions in some parts of the camp were already harsh, and even the Jews who were there to be exchanged did not live anything like a privileged life. Nevertheless, in 1944 conditions became even worse. A diminution of food and water supplies at the end of the year contributed towards a great rise in the previously comparatively low death rate. (The British liberators actually discovered a shed full of food, kept from the inmates, and there is of course no evidence that the guards went hungry.) The state of all the prisoners in Belsen deteriorated, not through hard labour as in many other camps but through neglect. In a matter of months the camp developed into the charnel-house we associate with the liberation of the concentration camps.

WOMEN ARRIVE FROM AUSCHWITZ-BIRKENAU

In the summer of 1944 the camp was expanded with the creation of a women's transit camp. In effect, this was an area of land adjacent to the

Star Camp where female forced labourers, transported from camps further east, lived in tents before moving on to the next factory. In the autumn other large transports of women arrived from Auschwitz-Birkenau. As newly erected barracks in the Star Camp were not yet ready, these women, too, were housed in tents. There were no sanitary arrangements and the tents were no protection from the rain or icy winds; one night a storm ripped them away. The women were then moved into a section of the Star Camp, although a barbed-wire fence prevented them from mixing with the other prisoners.

Along with the prisoners evacuated from Poland, the SS personnel who had administered the death camps were also relocated. Thus the changing character of Bergen-Belsen was sealed with the arrival in December 1944 of a new commandant, SS Captain Josef Kramer, previously in a position of command at the Auschwitz-Birkenau complex. He and the staff who accompanied him imposed a strict and vicious regime on the camp as a whole. They also failed to address the ever-worsening supply situation.

A NEW AND PUNISHING REGIME

Conditions in Belsen had deteriorated so greatly that hunger and illness affected the majority of prisoners. The onset of winter only worsened the situation. A punishing twice-daily roll call, where the prisoners had to gather to be counted in often terrible weather conditions, could last hours and took many lives. Disease became rife in the camp and eventually it became normal to see dead bodies piling up. Typhus spread like a forest fire in such conditions.

Belsen held 15,257 prisoners on Kramer's arrival. This number multiplied rapidly, however, as more and more evacuation transports rolled into Bergen railway station, carrying weak and starving prisoners. Prisoners were brought from all over Germany following chaotic routes often targeted by Allied bombing raids. In March Mr Abisch endured a typical journey from Dora to Belsen, with little food and and water, which lasted eight days in a cattle truck covered with tarpaulin. Paul Trepman was a member of a party taken to Belsen from a secret munitions plant in the Harz mountains in March 1945. For six days he and 4,000 others, with no food or room for movement, were hauled along a route that should have taken seven hours. Other prisoners were rounded up in Hanover and Hamburg, where they had been clearing bomb sites or working in factories, and literally dumped in Belsen.

The perimeters of the camp were physically expanded, yet Belsen could still not accommodate all the new arrivals. Conditions worsened further to an appalling degree. By 31 March 1945 there were 44,060 prisoners in Belsen, yet in that month alone it is thought that over 18,000 people died. An estimated 35,000 people lost their lives in the first three and a half months of 1945, before liberation, and the total death toll of the camp prior to liberation may have been as high as 45,000. Among them was Anne Frank, who died in February, probably of typhus.

The chaos of Germany in general was reflected in Belsen a hundredfold. Transports of weary and emaciated prisoners arrived at the camp with their SS guards and were turned away. Others were accepted. In the weeks preceding the liberation various transports of prisoners were evacuated to and from the camp, on balance increasing the population. It is thought that 7,000 people were on three trains that left (it is presumed) for Theresienstadt in Czechoslovakia in April. Many of those who left were replaced by prisoners marched on foot from the Neuengamme camp near Hamburg, evacuated in the face of advancing British troops. Likewise the Americans were closing in on the area around the Mittelbau-Dora sub-camp of Buchenwald concentration camp, and many of the prisoners evacuated from there – over 25,000 – descended on Belsen. These thousands could not possibly have been accommodated in the main camp and were taken to the barracks of a Panzer training school just over a mile away.

Unlike other concentration camps, Belsen was not generally evacuated, nor were the prisoners murdered *en masse*. This was pursuant to the logic of Himmler's negotiations in 1944 over exchanging some Hungarian Jews for goods or money. One of his motivations in this process was the possibility of opening up a channel of communication with the Allies in the interests of a negotiated peace, and also of presenting himself as mitigating the Jewish plight. Therefore Himmler gave the German military clearance to hand the camp over to the British forces, with no guarantees given in return about the treatment of the SS camp guards.

THE LIBERATION

When the British soldiers liberated Bergen-Belsen on 15 April they found a camp rife with typhus, containing emaciated prisoners of all nationalities. Among them were many Jews, Poles and political prisoners and a smaller number of Sinti (Romany) prisoners. Beyond those tens of thousands who had already died in the camp, a further 13,000 would die in the ensuing days and weeks as a result of their condition on liberation. In the words of one survivor, although fewer people died in Bergen-Belsen than in Birkenau, death was more visible: 'In Birkenau entire groups would simply disappear...In Bergen-Belsen...you died slowly, from illness, exhaustion, cold, most of them from hunger...In Bergen-Belsen you stared death in the face at every moment.'[6]

NOTES

1. Peter Longerich, *Politik der Vernichtung: Eine Gesamtdarstellung der nationalsozialistischen Judenverfolung* (Munich: Piper, 1998).
2. E. Kolb, *Bergen-Belsen: From 'Detention Camp' to Concentration Camp, 1943–1945*, 2nd rev. edn (Göttingen, 1986).
3. See Donald Bloxham, 'Jewish Slave Labour and its Relationship to the "Final Solution"', in John K. Roth and Elizabeth Maxwell (eds), *Remembering for the Future: the Holocaust in an Age of Genocide* (Basingstoke: Macmillan, 2001), Vol. 1, pp. 163–86.
4. Richard Breitman, 'Himmler and Bergen-Belsen', in Jo Reilly et al. (eds), *Belsen in History and Memory* (London: Frank Cass, 1997), p. 82; Alexandra-Eileen Wenck, *Zwischen Menschenhandel und 'Endlösung': Das Konzentrationslager Bergen-Belsen* (Paderborn: Ferdinand Schöningh, 2000), passim.
5. See Kolb, *Bergen-Belsen*, pp. 20–1; Bernard Wasserstein, *Britain and the Jews of Europe 1939–1945* (Oxford: Clarendon Press, 1979).
6. W. Lindwer, *The Last Seven Months of Anne Frank* (New York: Pantheon Books, 1991), pp. 105–6.